Shaggy Dogs & Other Stories

Shaggy Dogs
& Other Stories

Tales of a Kiwi Vet

David Marshall

SHOAL BAY PRESS

DEDICATION

To Murray Atkinson

First published in 1997 by
Shoal Bay Press Ltd
Box 2151, Christchurch

ISBN 0 908704 69 0

Cover photograph: Author and Lynn Brown's Ike, by Lloyd Park
Line drawings by Judy Lawn

Reprinted June 1998
Printed by Brebner Print

Contents

1. First Day as a Vet   9
2. The Beginning of an Idea   13
3. Bombs, Bees and Binder Twine   18
4. The Student Life   33
5. Back to the West Coast   54
6. More Wild West Adventures   77
7. Small is Better   94
8. The Longest House Call   116
9. A Home of Our Own   129
10. Leaving Maffeys Road   143
11. Out On Our Own   150
12. Of Leopards and Lions   173
13. Ducks, Fish … and Franz Kafka   183
14. Flicking the Switch   191

AUTHOR'S NOTE

Thanks to family, friends and colleagues for their forebearance and support during the writing of this book. Many of them feature as themselves in these stories in the expectation, well, hope, that they will forgive me. All other names and pertinent details have beeen changed to protect the privacy of the individuals concerned.

1

First Day as a Vet

The road curved seductively ahead of me in the washed, sparkling West Coast sunshine as I eased my brand-new Peugeot into the bend. The boot was immaculately laid out with compartments for sterile instruments, syringes, calving gear and drugs. There was a place in one corner for muddy gumboots.

'Never leave your shoes on the ground,' Vince had warned me. 'The dogs'll piss on them.'

I raised a finger in respectful greeting as I passed a farmer checking his letterbox. I felt more like brandishing my whole arm out the window and screaming, 'I'm the new vet!'

The barest twitch of a rigidly disciplined finger was his response.

Kelly, my little dog, settled herself more comfortably into a position between my leg and the armrest on the door.

'No more than you deserve, my girl, after the penury of student life,' I told her.

I was on my way to Fox Glacier to remove a cancerous eye from a Hereford cow. The disease is caused by an unpigmented eyelid's exposure to sunlight and most farmers cull cows with this problem.

A group of men was waiting at the yard as I pulled in.

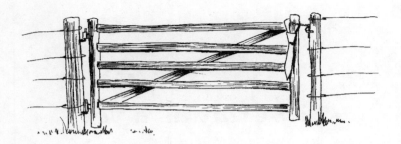

'Best-dressed gate on the Coast.'

'Gidday. I'm Vern Reilly,' said one of them, stepping forward to shake my hand. 'And you must be the new vet.'

I became conscious of the creases in the legs of my overalls and the obscene slickness of my new gumboots as I put them on. I took my tie off and hung it on a gate.

'Best-dressed gate on the Coast!'

I laughed obediently.

'Anyway, Doctor,' he went on with an extravagant gesture, 'come and meet your patient.'

He thought he was going to impress me and he did. The cow was huge. Her withers were just visible over the top rail, her belly pressed on both sides of the race and she had to tilt her head sideways to accommodate her horns. The tumour had eroded the entire upper eyelid and was growing across the eyeball. As they forced her into the head bale I collected the sterile instruments and drugs from the car, turning away to conceal my shaking hands as I filled the syringe with Pentothal. By some miracle I managed to find the jugular vein in her tree trunk of a neck and administered the anaesthetic. For an agonising moment nothing happened, then her huge body slumped abruptly to the ground.

'Hey, open the gates! Open the gates!' I yelled, stepping back into the tray of sterile instruments that I'd placed ready on the grass and tipping them all out. Nobody seemed to notice as they wrestled to pull the huge gate open just in time for this enormous cow to crash sideways onto the ground.

A flicker of admiration crossed Vern's face.

Exciting stuff, this veterinary medicine, I thought to myself as I surreptitiously cleaned the mud off the instruments.

'Keep that head stretched out,' I ordered, feeling slightly more in charge. I had just started to shave up the eyelid to prepare the area for the operation when the cow began to struggle.

That's funny, I thought. I'd calculated the dose of Pentothal very carefully and I'd injected it in one bolus, so I knew that I had time to get the operation over.

'She must be waking up.'

I stopped and filled up another syringe to deepen the anaesthetic, but just as I was ready to inject it the cow gave a bubbling groan and pink fluid ran from her mouth. Her back arched, her hind legs extended and she stopped breathing.

'Jesus Christ!' said the owner, piously.

Feverishly I leapt up and down on the enormous cow's chest in what I vainly hoped would pass for artificial respiration, but inexorably, her eyes glazed and went dull.

'You've killed her, mate, you've killed her!' he said, 'Christ! Can you do mouth to mouth?'

'No,' I said, weakly.

But when he flung himself on the ground and stuck his lips up one of her nostrils I was forced to go on jumping up and down on the chest, even though I knew it was futile. Eventually he conceded that the cow was irrevocably dead. He stood up and stared at me accusingly with haggard eyes, cow snot dripping from his unshaven mouth.

'This has been a very expensive experiment,' he said. 'That cow was the nucleus of my breeding stock. Are you a proper vet, or are you still a student?'

So much for the excitement, charm and charisma of being a vet. My childhood dreams had not covered this eventuality. Nor did it seem to be the right moment to tell Mr Reilly that cancer eye was an inheritable disease and the cow should not have been bred from anyway. All I could do was gather my equipment together, put it in the back of my as-yet-unpaid-for Peugeot, call off Kelly, who had started to sniff around the carcass in anticipation of an enormous meal, and drive dejectedly back to Hokitika.

What on earth ever gave me the idea that I wanted to be a vet?

2

The Beginning of an Idea

Mum and Dad both left school during the Depression at about the age of 12 to work on farms, Dad down in Southland and Mum in North Canterbury. After they married they bought a house in Linwood, an eastern suburb of Christchurch.

The houses were ageing villas – large, well built and freezing in the winter. They had big sections, at least a quarter of an acre, with well-established gardens and often orchards. For Dad, the fact that there was room to build his own workshop was reason enough to live in Linwood, but it was the trees that attracted Mum. Bottling fruit, picking berries and producing a mountain of veges was her passion. There was also a large collection of elderly neighbours for her to take care of with the surplus.

Let me tell you about my mother. She was short but in my mind she towered over me. She was fat but had the tenacity of a marathon runner. She had an unwavering, unflagging determination to achieve what she wanted. And what she wanted was for her three sons to make something of their lives. She didn't care what it was as long as it was an achievement, as long as it was an effort. She believed in hard work.

Even as an adult, if I heard Mum's footsteps coming into the house I would leap to my feet and look around to see what I should have been doing. She had the ability to make me feel guilty even on the rare occasions that I was innocent.

She said she was happiest in the company of males, which wasn't unexpected since she was the only girl in a family of four and she herself had three sons and no daughter. If anyone was equipped to nurture and rear boys, my mother was. She spent some time working at the Kingslea Girls' Correction Centre and imagined herself to be quite tough; and she was. She was suspicious of the motives of women, the girls at the correction centre having left her with the impression that women set out to get pregnant and trap themselves a man. We were often warned of this possibility.

Mum developed high blood pressure quite early in her life, and made very little effort to keep it under control. She died of a stroke in her mid-sixties.

My brothers will disagree with me but I think Dad was at his best when, after a lifetime of smoking, he was dying of emphysema. He said that dying didn't concern him in the slightest, as long as there was no pain attached to it. I asked him if he wanted a minister, but his lifetime atheism didn't waver.

'Don't be so bloody stupid,' he said.

Towards the end – and he was only really sick for a week – the nurses wanted to give him a bath. Even after sitting up it took about half an hour before he recovered his breath, so he thought a bath was out of the question.

'Look,' he said, 'leave me now, but I'll tell you what. In a day or two I'll get the undertaker to give me a decent scrub-up.' And he did.

Dad was a courageous, moral, disciplined, fierce, angry man with eyebrows that obscured his vision and moved alarmingly about his face. As a younger man he'd been a builder and knocked some teeth out with a hammer. If he didn't have his dental plate in his mouth, when he was angry – and he became angry frequently – his face would distort into a hideous grimace, displaying great black gaps where his teeth were missing.

When I was a student at Massey University I had a girlfriend for a short time who was the daughter of the then Minister of Education. I was naive enough not to know who her father was, and when I asked what he did she said that he was a beef breeder, being too embarrassed to tell me the full facts of his life. I was equally embarrassed to tell her the full facts of my father's life, i.e. that he was a budgie breeder, the secretary of the Carpet Workers' Union and an enthusiastic socialist.

Now I have nothing but admiration for him. I admire him as a soldier who, after being captured on Crete, escaped and lived rough in the mountains until he finally crossed the island to the other side, where he was taken off by submarine and went back to fight again. I admire him for the fact that when he came home on leave he refused to go back to the war along with the rest of them. I love the way he would stick his head out of the car window and refer to drivers who interfered with his mad path across town as 'besoms'.

But this is an adult view. As a child I was mostly terrified of him. He once whipped me with the ironing cord so hard that it drew blood and left a scab across my bottom for about two weeks. Mind you, that was only a week longer than the scabs we received from the cane at school, so I suppose that relatively it wasn't too harsh.

One of my earliest recollections of my father is of his hideously distorted face as he raised the sledgehammer to smash the little enamel potties that he had kicked over under our beds for the final time. Mum's protests that we were only three and four years old and that the outside toilet was too much for us in the dark meant nothing against his anger. I still remember peeping out of the window at these flattened piles of tin and watching the enamel ping off the surfaces of them, as he stalked off.

He bought me a little bicycle when I was about four – a tiny frail thing which I quickly mastered so I no longer needed the trainer wheels. As Dad was always on night shift I decided to undertake their removal myself. Unfortunately I didn't stop there, and after about two hours of mechanicking I'd reduced the bike to its larger component parts, with screws and nuts and other small pieces all lost around me in the grass.

When Dad discovered this he happened to be bringing in an armload of firewood, so he chased me down Hereford Street for more than 100 yards, throwing firewood at me until he ran out.

Dad was a plain, uncomplicated man. He thought both Rob Muldoon and the churches were self-seeking and self-serving, and whenever Muldoon appeared on television he would become so enraged he would spit and bite his thumb until it bled. He had nothing but contempt for inherited wealth and finally was even slightly contemptuous of wealth derived from hard work. He reserved any respect or admiration that he had in him for those who could do things.

Dad's workshop was a Mecca for us and a sanctuary for him. It was equipped with every piece of woodworking gear imaginable. He had come home from the war and, after they were married, Mum had taken charge of him. She sent him to an army rehabilitation course to train as a carpenter and builder, and this became his occupation. He did his own joinery and had a saw bench, a lathe, a buzzer (which finally cut his fingers off), a drill press and endless numbers of hand tools, which he patiently taught us to use.

He was an inveterate hoarder, perhaps as a result of his childhood during the Depression, when there was never enough so nothing was ever thrown away.

'Might come in handy some day,' he would say.

Screws were taken out of woodwork, hinges were saved, nails were pulled out and hammered straight. He pushed so much wood into the rafters of the garage that the whole thing collapsed, trapping the Morris 10 inside. He saved Brylcream bottles and nailed the lids to the rails, screwing the bottles in and out under them, so that all the different-sized screws, nails and hinges he had collected could be sorted and stored.

Everywhere he went Dad collected. A trip to the dump usually meant that he brought home more stuff than he took. I remember being embarrassed because he had a stand-up row with the dump's bulldozer driver, who accused him of scavenging. The argument was only resolved after the driver manoeuvred his bulldozer right next to Dad's car, threatening to run it completely over. Dad bit his knuckle through to the bone that day.

When we were quite young, Dad hurt his back and was no longer able to continue his trade as a builder. He took a job at the Riccarton Carpet Factory, working night shift, and for the rest of his working life and for the greater part of our childhood he slept during the day. When we were home he was asleep and we were very careful not to wake him up. Inevitably we grew apart from him and relied more on Mum.

3

Bombs, Bees and Binder Twine

Many people struggle as children because they cannot believe they're capable of achieving anything. Perversely, I suffered from the delusion that I could do absolutely anything. I only had to read about something and my mind immediately began constructing the image – glossing over the difficult bits of course. No sooner was the mental framework in place than my physical body would move in. I used to read Superman comics avidly, with the result that I would jump from high places in my gumboots with my army blanket cape draped around my shoulders, looking behind me to see if the cape fluttered correctly. The gumboots worried me a bit, because they didn't fit me round my calves the way Superman's did. So I tied binder twine around the tops to make them conform to my skinny little legs. My Superman adventures came to a sudden halt after I jumped off the coalshed roof, which was 20 feet high. Luckily the cape caught in the roof and stopped my fall.

On Friday nights Dad would take me to the Linwood Library, a real event for me. It was a gracious old building with a fire crackling in the grate to keep the pensioners warm and a kindly old chap with

I suffered from the delusion that I could do absolutely anything.

grey hair sitting in a glassed-in cubicle who would take your books back and issue new ones.

On each visit I would take out three or four of the children's educational books, such as books about rice and how paper was made. My father's Morris 10 had a light that shone on to the shelf under the passenger's part of the dashboard, so I would usually have read one of these books by the time I got home. By the time I got to primary school I was already able to read.

Dad was an avid book collector and would arrive home with heaps of books he'd got from second-hand shops. I read Homer's O*dyssey* when I was seven or eight. But Ellery Queen's mystery magazines were more of a favourite, and every time I got started on these books I could see myself in the hero's role.

We went to see the movie *Geordie* when we were quite small. It was about a big raw-boned Scotsman who became so proficient at throwing the hammer that he was picked for the Olympic Games. The actual details didn't concern us too much, but this idea of throwing the hammer was fascinating. The very next day we were out into the back yard practising throwing the broom, which was the nearest thing we had to a hammer. We became quite successful, until Geoff Paston threw it through the back of Dad's workshop which was built out of fibreboard: it was serviceable but a bit fragile. Luckily, he was away at work, so we spent the whole day putting a new piece back in before muddying it all up and writing our initials on it so he wouldn't find out. He never did.

Dad bought a garden hose at a cheap price from the chap over the road who worked at the rubber factory. We discovered that if you turned the hose on and pointed it directly at the ground the water washed the soil away and made a hole. Then, if you put the hose into the hole it washed more soil away, making the hole even deeper. We were able to push about 15 feet of hose into the ground using this method but when we turned the water off the ground settled around the hose so tightly that it was stuck there permanently. I remember staying well out of Dad's way as he tried to pull the hose out of the ground. He finally had to give up and cut it off.

When we were young, the Maynards were my brothers' and my worst enemies and during the 1950s the battle of Gallipoli was re-fought in our back yard. Graham Maynard is actually a good friend now, and he tells me that he thought we looked more like Turks than they did. They lived diagonally behind us, with their house on Cashel Street and ours on Hereford Street, and we had front-line trenches in both yards. A derelict chook house in no man's land became a burnt-out monastery. (Historical accuracy didn't concern us too se-riously.) Most of the battles involved hurling clods of dirt across the fence lines into each other's trenches. When they hit the ground they shattered like hand grenades.

This was until Dad discovered Urlwin's dump, beside the Heath-cote River in Opawa. Urlwin's was a large plastics manufacturer in Christchurch about that time, and Dad could fossick there for hours without the intrusion of officialdom. We followed soon after like chickens behind a bantam. Every Saturday Mum packed us a lunch with bottles of drink and sandwiches and off we'd go to the dump. It was a place with willows overgrowing the stream and ragwort pok-ing up through all the rubbish and junk. Most of the stuff there was reject plastic material, so we had hundreds of salt and pepper shakers at home. But occasionally real treasures turned up, like an enormous flywheel, so heavy that putting it on the carrier of the bike and riding home with it made the tyre pinch against the rim and flatten. It was no use to us but we thought it might 'come in handy' for Dad.

One of our treasures was a lady's bike that we took home and, by cutting up the frame, manufactured a bazooka. Brother Ken, being the youngest and only a lance corporal, became the aimer. His job was to hold the end of the tube against his chest and point it at the Maynards. I, as the colonel, grieving over the loss of so many fine men, had the job of lighting a skyrocket and dropping it down the end of the barrel. There would be a great WHOOSH! and a hole would suddenly appear in Ken's jersey, with the rocket spiralling er-ratically off across the fence.

We were the first with this sort of ammunition, and in the end we actually won the war with our bazooka, because one of our rockets struck the roof of the Maynards' house, setting fire to it. It took the whole Maynard family, with a bucket brigade, to put the fire out. At that point the parents got together and decided this was no longer a harmless weekend pursuit, so an armistice was signed.

Our successful experiments with the rocket got us interested in bombs. The method of construction was our own invention and the mechanism to explode the bombs was downright ingenious and, even by today's standards, relatively safe.

Mr Feswell, the neighbour at the back of us, had given us a pestle and mortar, a treasured old pottery thing, which we used to grind up the gunpowder we had acquired by various devious means. All the time we were grinding, sparks would fly: we thought this was wonderful.

The bomb was made out of two containers. The inner one contained the gunpowder and inserted through holes in the lid and into the gunpowder was a coil of nichrome wire – the wire that glows red hot in heaters. That was carefully insulated by two little pieces of plastic that we cut off some plastic wiring. The idea of the outer container was that as the gunpowder ignited and turned into gas, the pressure would build up much more than with just a little thin container, and the plaster of paris that we poured around the inner container would, we reasoned, increase this effect.

As it turned out, our theories proved to be spectacularly correct. The bombs were a resounding success. We started with smallish ones just buried in the ground and the bang was enormous. Every time we let one off, neighbours would rush out thinking there had been a car accident. We soon became more ambitious and decided to make one in a 25-pounder shell case that I imagined Dad had brought home from the war, but which I'm sure now wasn't the case. This bomb followed the same principle, except that amongst the plaster we'd added gravel.

We thought that this mighty weapon needed a really a good setting, so we dug a hole about four feet deep in the empty section next door – our Nevada Desert, if you like. Dad's battery charger was the power source. It had two little crocodile clips on it, which we had to replace every time we let off a bomb. One of these clips was put on each of the wires that stuck out of the top of the bomb. The 25-pounder shell case, filled with its gunpowder and plaster of paris and gravel, was lowered down the shaft. We then tamped earth all around it and crouched down behind the paling fence.

I leaned forward and flicked the switch.

For a moment nothing happened, but when it did the bang was magnificent. Even more impressive was the sustained torrent of gravel, boulders and rubble that rained down on us and the house straight afterwards.

Mum was a stoical sort of a person. At the time she had the lady from the Seventh Day Adventist church visiting. I don't think Mum was at all interested in what the poor woman had to say, but she was too kind-hearted to tell her to go away.

They had just made themselves comfortable with their cups of tea when the bomb went off. Mum casually sipped at her tea as this huge cacophony crashed and reverberated around the house.

' Good God, what on earth was that?' said the lady from the church.

'Don't worry, it's just the boys letting off bombs.'

I always thought our crowning achievement in this area of scientific endeavour was the bomb that we let off underwater. One of us had read somewhere that bombs exploded far more powerfully underwater than in the air, so to test this we made a really tiny bomb – tiny on account of the fact that the water was going to be held in Mum's rubbish tin.

Now Mum had, in what was a fairly impecunious neighbourhood, a unique social symbol, a Parker rubbish tin. Everyone else had sacks, old 40-gallon drums or buckets but Mum possessed a proper Parker rubbish tin with the label on the top and a lid. When the rubbish truck came to empty it they always looked after it very carefully and invariably placed the lid back on, in sharp contrast to the neighbours' old kerosene tins which were bashed all over the place.

We knew that if we asked permission we wouldn't be allowed to use Mum's rubbish tin, so we thought it would probably be all right as long as we were very careful. We chose a tiny 35-mm film cassette to hold the gunpowder and used a little Elastoplast tin as the outer case to ensure the charge would be relatively weak. We smeared the bomb and its leads with vaseline with the aim of stopping the water from leaking in, so the electricity would work properly. We placed Mum's rubbish tin exactly in the centre of the testing ground next door, filled it with water, and put a pipe across the top to suspend the bomb squarely in the middle.

Once again we crouched down behind the fence, each of us peering through his own knothole. I leaned forward and flicked the switch. Nothing happened for about a minute and it really looked as though the water had got in and we were seeing our first failure. Suddenly there was a muffled boom, and a wall of water shot across the empty section, splashing up the fence.

The rubbish tin had completely disappeared. The biggest piece we could find was about an inch across.

The only way to deal with the situation was to avoid talking about it altogether. When Mum said that thieves must have taken her rubbish tin, or that jealous neighbours had thrown it away, we could only look sideways at each other and nod guiltily.

When Neil Andrews rang to ask whether our bombs would be able to demolish a bees' nest we were only too keen to oblige. Apparently the bees were in the middle of a hollow cherry tree in his parents' garden. We made a moderate-sized bomb, nothing too spectacular, with the usual system of wires to make it go off. We took Dad's battery charger and the bomb around to Neil's place and lowered the device down into the bees' nest very carefully, irritating them only mildly in the process. We could see the cherry tree from the garage, where we had connected the battery charger up to the power. We flicked the switch and waited.

Now as a kid I always had a problem with being a bit secretive. I was inclined to think that I'd be told off, so didn't actually announce what I was going to do. In this case it was unfortunate, because immediately after we flicked the switch, Neil's mother came out of the kitchen door. She was standing in the sun admiring her garden when the bomb exploded. Directly before her eyes her beautiful old gnarled cherry tree, resplendent in full spring blossom, collapsed in a heap to the ground. The bomb had completely cut it in half.

The bees, however, had merely vibrated with the explosion – they were very angry and not at all dead. We were quite safe from them in the garage, but poor Mrs Andrews was not. She knew we were involved; she was yelling our names even through the pain of the bee stings. Mrs Andrews has never forgiven us for our bee-killing efforts and even now looks askance when she sees me.

If we had continued making bombs I feel sure we would have become more sophisticated and our safety record might have been exemplary. But the disaster came – and it was a disaster – when my brother John decided to make rockets. He'd fashioned a pointed end on a short length of conduit pipe that could be unscrewed for filling with gunpowder. Braised onto the other end was a little nipple that allowed a fuse to be pushed into the gunpowder. When he lit this rocket, suitably set up in the back garden, nothing happened. So he unscrewed the front end, emptied the gunpowder out and then attempted to undo the braising by heating it. The small residue of gunpowder in the pipe exploded, splitting the pipe along its seam so that it folded back over his fingers, resulting in the loss of the ends of four fingers and a thumb.

When I arrived home the family had all gone off to hospital. I thought there was something wrong, but I didn't know exactly what until I went out to the workshop and found the piece of pipe with the digits still stuck in it. By the time the police had arrived I had removed the pipe, so they decided that he must have caught his fingers in the drill press. It was a sad and traumatic period.

My mother's pronouncement on the whole episode was that she would rather we blew our fingers off than caught VD in the Square.

Linwood Park, just behind the primary school that we all attended, was the centre of our social activities, where we played soccer and attended the Labour Day picnic. There was a pond in the middle of the park where we could hunt for frogs and tadpoles, and Dad made a boat for us to sail on it.

The very last house on Randolph Street, which ran off the back of Linwood Park, was owned by the Smitherams, who were friends of ours. I played soccer with Ken and his brother Gary was John's age. One afternoon, when Mum was sick in bed with high blood pressure, we went round to the Smitherams' on our bikes to ride on the track they had built on the vacant council land behind their house. This was a child's version of the Aranui speedway track – a dirt circle around which a gang of small boys pedalled as fast as they could.

Inevitably there were arguments. Gary Smitheram took my brother John's bike off him and wouldn't give it back. Now John is a mild, rational, controlled person, more so than either of his two brothers. But on this occasion he was overcome by the Marshall temper so he reached down and picked up something to throw. It happened to be a spark plug, and the spark plug happened to stick into the back of Gary Smitheram's head. When it fell out, a huge gout of blood followed it. We quickly gathered up our bits and pieces, including the bike that had been in contention, and went home.

We didn't say anything to Mum, but went straight to the bedroom we shared. Shortly after, the supporters of Gary Smitheram – his brothers and the other kids from the street – turned up and began throwing stones on the roof, so we had to confess to Mum what had happened. She gave me a note to take to Mrs Smitheram, and after all the Randolph Street boys had left I climbed on my bike and went back to Linwood Park, cautiously approaching her house. There was a large tree in the park, so I hid behind it and peered out at Randolph Street, only to see a militia of Gary's supporters all training their air rifles at me. As the airgun pellets started pinging off the sides of the tree I realised that I wasn't welcome, so I turned around and went home again. Mum's blood pressure had not improved by the time I reached the house.

One of our regular Saturday morning expeditions was to bike to the Linwood railway station with our lunches and our fishing rods and catch a train that would take us through the Lyttelton tunnel so we could spend the day fishing at Cashin Quay, which in those days was being filled and was just a big pile of rocks. There was good fishing there though. I remember catching a 5lb kahawai and carting it in triumph all the way back in the train.

Occasionally we would fish off Gladstone Wharf, which acted as a breakwater to Lyttelton's inner harbour. My brother could cast so far that he could hit the inter-island ferry on its way out to Wellington. We spent a lot of time poking around the wharf area at Lyttelton, and our only difficulty with the law came during this time. Geoff Morrison and John Knowles had come with us – perhaps that was the reason for our trouble. After finding the fishing no good we started throwing stones at a collection of fibreboard markers set up on posts to tell the trucks where to dump rocks. It was pleasing to discover how easily they broke when hit with a stone, and we had been doing this for half an hour when a Land Rover pulled up and the driver got out.

We only really noticed him after he had put on a policeman's helmet. He called us over. Geoff Morrison and my brother ran away but when the policeman yelled out 'Stop!' they dutifully came back. He ordered us all into the back of the Land Rover and took us down to the police station, where we sat for half an hour until the sergeant arrived. He gave us a right old telling off, which we would have accepted quite happily if he hadn't said we were nothing but a bunch of hoboes.

John Knowles thought he said 'homos' and was seized with an unfortunate fit of giggles. It was probably nervousness, but the sergeant went absolutely berserk. Our parents were phoned and when we arrived home Mum, with tears rolling down her face, sat us down in the kitchen and cut off all our hair. Justice had been done. She said that if we wanted to behave like criminals we should look like criminals.

Mum decided that I should be a veterinarian and, although I was only ten years old, that was more or less that. The choice was inspired. From then on all my holiday jobs, all my spare-time activities revolved around becoming a vet. For example, Mum used her considerable influence as the tea lady at a large insurance office to place me in a prominent horse-training stables for more or less the whole of one school holiday. The following Christmas holidays she had me out boarding with Uncle Aubrey, Mum's brother, and his wife Florrie, who arranged for me to spend time at the Darfield Veterinary Clinic.

My uncle and aunt had lost a son in the polio epidemic so, thinking back, it was brave of them to take in a boy about their own son's age, only a few years after his death. They put me up in his bedroom, which was just as he had left it. There was a complete collection of William books, a double bed with a great big billowy feather mattress and a lovely eiderdown.

I was quite happy to be sent off to bed early every night because I could read the William books. There must have been 20 of them, which I devoured in about a week. Then, with nothing else to read, I discovered *The Farmer's Medical and Health Dictionary*. This was much more interesting than the William books and I read it night after night, intrigued by the range of diseases that could afflict mankind.

I discovered a condition called onanism. No details were given of this affliction except that it apparently occurred in young males. The most fascinating part was that the worst possible precipitating factor was feather mattresses. The treatment was to compel the patient to take frequent cold baths and to sleep in a very hard bed. The book emphasised that slats should be placed under the bed wire and only thin kapok mattresses be used. So here I was, ten years old, cocooned in this beautiful feather mattress, completely warm and cosy, waiting to be stricken with onanism. It was not until I was at Canterbury University that the disease finally struck me.

The vet clinic at Darfield was not going to be a place where a ten-year-old would gather a great deal of specific information, but I was enchanted by the atmosphere and mood of the place. There was a mixed aroma of cows' innards and disinfectant about the building, because they did all their own post mortems. There were strange-looking instruments, equipment and drugs, all very foreign and exciting to me, but the one thing that sticks in my memory was a box of beautiful blue insulin syringes with a striking bottle-blue central plunger. I coveted one of these syringes, almost to the point of stealing it. Several times I remarked casually to the vet, 'What a nice thing it is,' but he seemed to miss the point. Perhaps he was concerned I would become a drug addict overnight.

Years later, when I finally graduated and started practice, I recalled the fixation I had with the blue syringe, with the result that I now hand out disposable plastic syringes to everybody's children. I call them water pistols and I am sure they are all used as such. Perhaps some child holds on to his syringe and feels the same way I did.

Brian McLeavey and David Wood were the vets at Darfield during those holidays and I am very grateful for the time they gave me, although after all these yearse I can only recall Brian sewing up his own cut finger and David taking huge pleasure from driving over the humps in the road so fast that the car became airborne. I still see Brian periodically because he also practises in Christchurch, and I enjoy hearing his unique views on people and pets.

One of the best things Mum did was to encourage us to look after pets from when we were quite young. She was an animal lover herself and we had all sorts. First came the chooks. Beautiful, big Rhode Island Reds and Black Orpingtons scratched under the fruit trees in the back garden. Then Biddy the bantam arrived. We were allowed to take her to school in her box when she had her chickens and would proudly let the other children handle her babies. She once pecked my brother in the eye, but I think he might have been mean to her.

We had a hut called the bottle shed as part of a sizable collection of outhouses on the property. There was also a washhouse with an artesian well and an outside toilet. Separate again was the coal shed, while a much larger shed along the east fence was Dad's workshop, which I have already described. Fowl houses were later built along the back fence from car cases. But the bottle shed was our domain, even if Mum did keep all her preserving jars in there.

It was also the site for our first museum. We had a sign out on the road advertising it and we stood beside it, inviting people in. The number of people who turned up surprised Mum, especially as she had no idea that the museum existed. Our best exhibit was a comprehensive collection of birds' nests with eggs. We had thrushes, sparrows, blackbirds, yellowhammers, ducks, pukekos and starlings, each nest representing a perilous climb. We learned to blow the yolks out of the eggs through a hole made in each end. This was successful if they were collected early enough so there was no chicken inside, but even if there were a chick inside we still kept it, as the egg was too valuable to be left behind.

It was of no concern to us that the bottle shed developed a strange smell; each nest was carefully labelled and the eggs placed inside. The museum lasted about a week until Biddy the bantam decided that this would make an ideal place to add her nest and scraped all the existing nests and eggs into a heap and laid bantam eggs on top.

The museum died a natural death, but as a result of our burgeoning scientific interest Mum and Dad gave us a microscope. They lived just above subsistence level in an old house with an old car, so a microscope probably represented a Christmas holiday to them, but Mum thought it would be all worthwhile when we could show her a paramecium. We were all still very young, but we had read about these flagellate protozoa – tiny, swimming bugs that lived in puddles. She was as excited as we were to collect some water and see them with the microscope.

The bottle shed was also the place I chose for a gas mask testing operation. A friend of the family, Alan Baker, had bought up some World War II gas masks. They were made of rubber, completely enclosing the face with big glass goggles, with a corrugated pipe that hung down from the middle of the mask to a canister. I was intrigued to discover how these worked, so I shut myself in the little bottle shed and set fire to a heap of sulphur that I had left over from making bombs. This made a very satisfying cloud of smoke which quickly filled the room. It wasn't until the smoke came out from under the door that Dad burst in, thinking the place had caught fire, only to see me crouched in the corner with my gas mask. He was nearly overcome with the fumes but I was perfectly safe, if a little unhappy that I'd had to crash land yet another Spitfire.

Just as I could see myself as Biggles or Superman, I could see myself as a vet. I could wear the white coat and the overalls, which in my ten-year-old's mind fitted me much better than Superman's gumboots. I was perfectly convinced that becoming a vet was a very simple process. In fact I thought it was an apprenticeship, because in our family it was commonly accepted that apprenticeships were the highest level of academic excellence. It was only when I started at high school that I discovered that being a vet involved going to university.

4

The Student Life

I began my university career at Canterbury University, down the other end of Hereford Street from where we lived, so my first days there were not too terrifying, even if I did suffer from moments of great trepidation about what a Linwood kid like me would encounter when I got to university.

Although I had had some good times at school, occasionally doing reasonably well, I had spent most of my time blundering along in a state of relative inattention, so I had a real fear that when I got to university I'd be confronted by people with foreheads about a foot high and huge intellects, and I would be shown up for the dummy that I was.

I was lucky that I could still attend the old university, which is now the Christchurch Arts Centre. It was a fabulous place with a wonderful atmosphere; when I first arrived I had the impression that all I had to do was lift up my arms and the knowledge would soak in through my pores. I loved the old Gothic cloisters and the beautiful buildings and the fact that it had been used as a university for such a long time.

The students had left a real mark on the place. You could look up into the ceiling of D Room and read 'Social Stokes, disease spreader' or know that down under the Great Hall Rutherford had performed his early physics experiments. The Great Hall itself was the venue for the annual dances for different societies such as the Chemistry Society, or ChemSoc as it was called, where you were served with punch made with absolute alcohol.

It soon began to dawn on me was that here were groups of people with widely divergent ideas. There were poets and lawyers and all sorts of people with different inclinations and views from those of my father, and even though I didn't get to speak intimately with many of these people I began to feel that life could be different; it didn't have to be mere drudgery. There was time to do things that didn't involve just making enough money to scrape by. Some students would even demonstrate and join protests just before exams, and I felt quite concerned for them as they seemed to be neglecting their education.

This sanctimonious air was destroyed when, two weeks before exams and with notably poor timing, I discovered girls. With all Mum's imprecations and dark warnings of wicked women, not to mention the fact that I'd gone to a boys' school and had only brothers, it was perhaps fortunate that I found myself attracted to girls at all.

The particular girl in question also lived in Hereford Street, about halfway between our place and the university in an area that was filled with student flats. Unfortunately Mum also travelled along Hereford Street to and from her cleaning job in the middle of the night at the post office, 'to pay for your education'. The little Austin 7 that we owned was unusual enough for her to recognise on her way into work at 3am on her motorised bicycle. She was appalled to discover it still there at 7am as she returned home.

I woke up in my girlfriend's small, dark bedroom with the blinds

I admired the way the toe of my shoe was nuzzling into one of the cups of her bra.

pulled. Clothes were littered around the floor, some of them mine. I admired the way the toe of my shoe was nuzzling into one of the cups of her bra. In the corner was a desk with books piled all over it. The bed itself was supported on all corners by more books. I stretched luxuriously. I had arrived. I was a proper student.

Into this tranquil, sinful scene suddenly burst my brother John in his school uniform. The Shirley Boys' High uniform is bright Cambridge blue. He stood at the end of the bed, his blazer and cap appearing to shimmer and pulsate with the moral outrage that I knew both Mum and the school's headmaster possessed in full measure.

'Mum says you're catching VD,' he announced, and marched out of the room.

The girl leapt up and got dressed. She didn't offer me any breakfast or even a cup of coffee. The hand that I extended was not shaken and she did not invite me to see her again.

Part-way through my first year of university studies Roy Bailey and his wife Jan opened a vet clinic in Worcester Street, again very close to where we lived. Mum was keen for me to spend some time at the clinic to be sure that veterinary science was what I wanted to do, so I called in to see them. This was the start of a long association, and the clinic soon became my second home. Roy was an intense, quick-thinking person, while his wife was much more methodical, and I soon found myself spending most of my recreational time at their place.

Mum used to say, 'You've got to pass first; don't just play at being a vet, you actually have to get the degree,' and of course she was right. But it was fascinating, it really was what I wanted to do. I loved the surgery; I loved the contact with people; I loved the feeling of making a difference in a unique job.

After I had spent some time helping him in the clinic Roy suggested I go and see a large animal practice in the summer holidays; he had a friend in Hokitika who might be able to help. This sounded like a great idea, so it was arranged that I would spend some time with Vince Peterson, who would meet me at the station.

I arrived in Hokitika about four or five on a Saturday afternoon. There was no one to meet me, but that didn't worry me too much, as I knew these were busy people. I heaved my pack on my back and walked around to 11 Hoffman Street, which was the Hokitika veterinary clinic, and found the vet's house beside it. It looked a bit like the sort of state house you might see today – the same beige colour, with the same tiled roof and the porch right in the middle of the front.

I knocked on the door. No answer. No sign of anybody at all. I was at a bit of a loss to know what to do, so I stood there for a while and finally decided that as the last couple of weeks camping in Nelson with my friends had been a bit hectic, I would unroll my sleeping bag, curl up on the front porch and go to sleep.

At about nine o'clock in the evening I was woken up by the clinking of bottles as three or four people walked into the house over the top of me, carrying crates of beer. They went inside and the door was shut. Then about ten minutes later someone stuck his head out the door and said, 'What's your name?'

I felt a bit silly lying on the floor of the porch with my head sticking out of my sleeping bag like a turtle, but I said, 'I'm Davey Marshall.'

'Oh, and what do you want?'

'I've come to see Vince Peterson. He was going to show me things about being a vet.'

'Oh, hang on.'

The door shut again, there was some urgent shuffling behind it and the head of Vince Peterson himself appeared. 'Hello,' he said. 'By God, man, I'd forgotten all about you. Never mind. Come on in, come on in. We thought you were some sort of a tramp.'

I scrambled out of my sleeping bag and shuffled into the light. He sat me down. 'Hey, Bill,' he said. 'get Davey Marshall a drink. We've just committed a terrible social gaffe.'

I was handed a bottle of beer and took a couple of cautious sips. 'Sorry about that,' he said. 'I just forgot completely about you. But tell me, man, do you drink?'

I remembered the two weeks at Nelson, shuddered a bit and said, 'Yes.'

'Oh, good,' he said. 'Do you smoke?'

At that time I did smoke quite enthusiastically, so was able to agree again.

'Ah,' he said. 'Well now, tell me, what about women?'

This was something I was not so familiar with, but I nodded. I didn't want to appear too foolish in front of these men.

'Good,' he said, 'In that case you can stay.'

So that was my introduction to Vince Peterson.

The next two weeks were the most strenuous I think I've ever put in. Not only did the drinking and the socialising continue at a furious pace, but the working and the exercising did as well.

If I ever needed a demonstration of the drama of veterinary practice, Vince provided it. We had been calving cows all day at Hari Hari when Charlie Evans's voice crackled over the radio telephone.

'Vetbase to one-seven-seven, do you receive? Over.' replied Vince.

'I've just had a call from the circus people in Westport. They want you up there straightaway. Three of their elephants have tutu poisoning.'

'Bloody hell,' said Vince. Turning to me he said, 'I think we'd better pick up Dick Lim to give us a hand with this.' Dick was a Malaysian vet who was working with Vince at the time.

'Does Dick know about elephants?' I asked naively.

'Only Lenny Larsen knows about elephants,' replied Vince darkly.

Even though they design Porsches, the makers of Volkswagens never meant Vince's little car to travel at the speeds he drove it. Westport is 180 kilometres north of Hokitika, and the trip took an hour and a half. I have never been so frightened in my life.

The circus had been set up at the racecourse. The big top was already up when we arrived, but inside was carnage. The locals had slashed the ear veins of all three elephants, as it was reputed to be an effective treatment against toot. They had also brewed up all the tea they could find and drenched the elephants with that – another local remedy that didn't seem to have worked.

Vince found the elephant trainer crouching beside one of his prostrate charges. 'Start from the beginning,' he said. 'What happened?'

The trainer was a small, wizened, wrinkled, red-faced man who weighed about seven stone. We later found out that a good part of his weight was composed of sherry. 'Well,' he said unsteadily, 'when we pull up, we usually get the elephants to unload these big steps here onto the ground beside the truck so that they can walk down. Well, Matilda put a foot on the top step and tipped arse over kite. This is her here – she's never got up since.'

The deck of the truck was covered in tutu leaves. 'Where do you reckon these came from?' said Vince.

'Oh, they must've come off the sides of the road on the way through the Buller Gorge. These girls just reached out and grabbed them and stuffed them in.'

Tutu poisoning causes diarrhoea, vomiting and convulsions, and these elephants had already exhibited all three signs. The piles of vomit were spectacular: they reached waist height.

'Well,' said Vince in despair, 'I'll tell you something for nothing. These three elephants are going to die. Toot is fatal.'

'I won't accept that,' said the manager, Joe, coming up behind Vince. 'We need another opinion.'

Vince said, 'Well, the best thing I can suggest is that you ring Lenny Larsen in Sydney, Australia. Here's his number.'

'Right,' said Joe, and stumbled off.

He came back a while later.

'Did you get hold of him?'

'Oh, yes,' said Joe, 'I found him.'

'What did he say?'

'Well, he started off by asking who was the vet I had on hand. When I told him your name, he said "Oh, Vince Peterson, I remember him. Yep, you've got a good man there".'

'What else did he say?' said Vince.

Joe hesitated. 'Well, he said that they were going to die, that toot is usually fatal. So I'm in your hands, Vince. Do everything you can.'

'Look at this girl here, Matilda,' the trainer broke in. 'She looks a bit bloated.'

'Oh,' Vince said. 'I can do something about that.'

He rushed off to his little Volkswagen, lifted up the bonnet and came back with a trocar – an instrument consisting of a central spike inserted down the middle of a tube. Vince climbed up the hay bales that had been placed beside the fallen elephant, scrambled on top of her, raised both hands in the air and lunged as hard as he could with his trocar. His arms bounced into the air as high as he had raised them. Ten further attempts produced the same result, so he gave up.

Dick Lim then said, 'I know they've been sick already, but if we were to make them even sicker they might bring all of the tutu up and that might help.'

'Okay,' said Vince. 'Anything. We'll try anything.'

All three of us went off to see the local chemist. 'What have you got to make an elephant sick?' asked Vince.

I could tell the chemist had never been asked this question before. 'Come out the back and we'll have a look,' he said.

This was an old chemist's shop with many redundant drugs in the storeroom. After about 20 minutes the chemist came up with some white powder in a bottle. 'This'll do it,' he said. 'Bismuth antimony tartrate makes people sick – kills them in fact.'

'Great,' said Vince. 'What about a dose?'

'You want a dose of this stuff for elephants?' asked the chemist dubiously. 'You won't find that in the *British Pharmacopoeia*, I imagine. Tell you what – I've got a dose for humans; why don't we just multiply it by the number of humans in a elephant?'

In the end Vince simply guessed. They mixed the medicine up in water and returned to the racecourse, where two of the elephants in the big top were still standing, piles of vomit and diarrhoea at front and back respectively, and puddles of blood below each ear. Matilda lay where we'd left her.

Vince placed a stepladder against one of the enormous beasts and climbed up beside the elephant's head. He finally found a vein that had not been slashed and slowly injected the Bismuth antimony tartrate. The result was instantaneous. The elephant vomited with Herculean vigour. He repeated the same treatment on the other two elephants, with the same result.

'I wonder if we got that girl to stand up,' said Vince. 'Do you think it would help?'

The little trainer came stumbling out of the darkness, smelling strongly of sherry. 'Well, we'll get Martha here to lift Matilda up with her trunk and tusks – they do that, you know,' he said.

'Right-ho,' said Vince, 'let's go.'

So they removed the shackle from Martha's leg. This was the opportunity Martha had been waiting for. Letting out two hair-raising screams of anger she trotted at full speed down the length of the big top.

But the trainer had clearly anticipated what was going to happen and had dug his long, spiked stick in behind Martha's ear. He hung on grimly and found himself whisked along the ground, his seven stone making very little difference to Martha's progress. At the end of the tent she simply burst through the canvas, leaving it tattered and torn behind her. With one final scream she disappeared into the darkness of Westport with the trainer still hanging on.

Twenty minutes later he limped back in. Apparently she had run the length of the racecourse, down a lane, and had just managed to negotiate a right-angled corner. The prick of the trainer's pole in her ear had finally infuriated her to a point when she swung mightily with her trunk to dislodge him. She succeeded in knocking 15 feet of corrugated iron fence to the ground beside her, and the trainer wisely decided at this stage to fall to the ground.

Joe rallied all available circus hands with the instructions that they were to find Martha. But, amazingly, she was not to be found. An enormous elephant was utterly lost within the small town of Westport.

Fred Foster had set his alarm early to go whitebaiting. When it rang he staggered out in the half light of 4am to have a pee in the back garden. His head thumped and he had difficulty focusing, but he felt huge relief as his bladder started to empty. He looked up toward the sky.

'Should be a good morning for whitebaiting. Tide'll be right soon. No wind. Garden doesn't look bad. Funny about that elephant eating the cabbages.' He looked again. No question – there *was* an elephant eating his cabbages.

Fred staggered inside and woke his wife. 'Joyce, come here, come here!'

'Oh, go away,' she said. 'Why don't you just go whitebaiting?'

'No,' he cried. 'Come and have a look in the garden. There's an elephant eating our cabbages.'

'Jesus Christ, Fred, that's the last bloody straw!' But she got up and confirmed that indeed there was an elephant eating the cabbages.

When Fred rang the police station they didn't believe him. They'd visited the pub the night before and knew what state he'd been in when he went home. They knew his reputation for drunkenness and the occasional bout of delirium tremens.

'Fred,' they said, 'we don't believe you. There's no such thing as an elephant loose in Westport.'

Fred finally had to speak to the police sergeant before he could convince them of the truth of his statement.

Martha was recaptured quite easily because elephants are docile, friendly animals in the main, except when they have been poisoned, cut to ribbons and injected with vomit-inducing chemicals. But happily the vomiting had worked, for all three elephants survived.

We drove home at a much more sedate pace in the morning. Vince turned to me and said, 'Do you still want to be a vet?'

One afternoon Vince and Dick Lim decided to have a push-ups competition. They would do them in twenties and the winner would buy the other more beer, of course. Fitness and training have never been part of my repertoire, but I thought I'd better join in. Vince did 84 push-ups, Dick Lim did about 80, and I managed about 50. The next morning my arms were so sore I couldn't get a piece of toast to my mouth. I couldn't do my shoes up, I couldn't even bend my elbows.

'Come on,' said Vince. I'll give you a hand to get dressed – we're off to the races.' It turned out he was the duty vet that day at the Hokitika races.

About the middle of the afternoon the swabbing steward, the person who was employed by the club to help the vet do his duty, had to go home to milk the cows, so Vince said not to worry, his friend, this veterinary student, would do the job. So they put me into a white coat and off we went.

Up to then my contact with horse people, especially racehorse people, had been limited, so I found the whole business rather astounding. It was a wet day, by no means rare on the Coast, and as I walked around the stables and in behind the racing scene I couldn't believe the number of thin, cold, shivering people who seemed to populate the racecourse. It seemed to me that the jockeys looked mean, cold and cynical; the boys, the grooms and stable hands looked underfed and under-loved, with a mistrusting, resentful view of the world.

Dealing with these people as though I were someone of importance proved difficult. From the moment the stipendiary steward said, 'We're going to swab this horse,' the swabbing steward had to remain with it to ensure that no water entered its mouth, and that no one interfered with it. When the result of the next race was announced the stipendiary steward said he wanted to swab the winner and Vince said, 'Go along, go with him.'

As the jockey was dismounting I walked up to him and said, 'Come on. We're going to swab this horse.'

The jockey said, 'Piss off, mate. It's nothing to do with me.'

I knew so little about horse racing that I had no idea that the jockey had to go and weigh his gear in, so he wouldn't remain in charge of the horse after he dismounted. But a stable boy turned up, grabbed the reins, and trotted the horse off across the yard.

'David, keep up with him, keep up with him!' Vince yelled out.

My body was so stiff from the exercise of the day before that all I could do was yell, 'I'm going as fast as I can' as they disappeared toward the stables.

I never did like the races.

When I arrived home after my fortnight with Vince I had no laces in my shoes and only one sock. It took a further week to get my arms to work properly and for the rest of my body to detoxify. My introduction to the West Coast and its people had been complete in one short break and I couldn't wait to get back.

Entry to vet school demanded a pass in chemistry, physics, zoology and botany. I passed everything except physics in my first year. In the second year at Canterbury I failed physics again, but had improved to a D. At the same time I managed to pass Stage 2 zoology and chemistry. In my third year I finally scooped the pool with a C in physics, Stage 3 zoology and another botany unit. At last I was accepted at the vet school in Palmerston North.

Vince Peterson had become my benefactor both at Canterbury and at Massey. I would write to him regularly to ask for loans to keep me in the lifestyle to which I had rapidly become accustomed, and he always very obediently obliged.

I had certainly made a radical change from my frugal childhood. My father thought that he had spawned an aristocrat and became quite disparaging about my social standing. With my first bursary at the vet school I bought an umbrella and a gold watch. The family were appalled and my brother John, who came up with the University of Canterbury shooting team to the Easter tournament at Massey, was expressly instructed to tell me that Dad disapproved of this gold watch business and I must take greater care with my funds. But by this time I had developed an attitude of total *laissez faire*.

'When I graduate,' I told John, 'I'll have so much money that paying off all these loans will be nothing.'

In fact, two years after I graduated my debt to Vince remained unchanged, so when after a period working with him on the Coast I shifted back to Christchurch to work for Roy, he paid Vince the five or six thousand dollars that I still owed, and I continued to pay Roy off. I preferred to think of it as transfer money – the sort of stuff that professional soccer players get.

The reason I had this enormous debt was that I lived a very good social life in Palmerston North. When I first arrived at the vet school I lived in one of the hostels, Colombo Hall, for a term. Towards the end of that term I was approached by Dick Dean, a classmate, who wanted to know whether I would be prepared to go flatting with him in the town. The hostels and the university itself were about seven or eight miles outside Palmerston North, but he had a car, which would be a distinct advantage. He was also used to flatting and the ways of the world, while I clearly was not.

I wrote a couple of letters to Mum and Dad offering, looking back on it, some very spurious arguments about needing to be away from the general fuss and bother of university hostels and completely disregarding the fact that it would cost more than the hostel. Transport would always be a problem, in spite of Dick's car, since I was no longer within walking distance of the library and the other facilities. The unwritten part of my reasoning – and I'm sure Mum realised this – was the fact that I was closer to the pubs and the distractions that reduced learning ability. However, looking back, it was a good move.

I flatted with Dick in a back flat at Pascal Street for four years. The flat had an electric heater at one end of the lounge, which we had framed with a big copper reflector and put a wooden bookcase round it. It looked very smart. Unfortunately Dick stuck his leg in the heater one day and received a sizable shock. His body did something we'd been studying in physiology: the shocked leg withdrew sharply, while the other leg extended just as sharply. It was called, in animals, the crossed extensor reflex, and I was fascinated to see it happening in a human. The fact that he kicked the heater to bits with his abrupt extension of the other leg was not appreciated by the landlord.

Norman was one of the few married students in the class and he and his wife Lois would often invite us around for tea. It was great to have a woman cook for us occasionally, because our own food was always a little basic, though Dick was quite a good cook. But we returned the favour and one night invited Norman's whole family for dinner. We prepared a huge meal – soup out of a can, followed by a roast with vegetables and potatoes, then ice-cream and fruit salad.

In the kitchen of our flat there was a little alcove where we had an agitator washing machine with a heater element in the bottom. We had bought the washing machine at an auction, along with a couple of beds, but we had only gone about 300 yards down the road when it fell off the trailer, sustaining a large dent in the side, as a result of which it was never very functional. But the washing machine was used during that first year to prepare the bones of a sheep's skeleton for anatomy. We'd visited a farm where we found suitably decomposing bones, which we put in the washing machine to remove all the wool and bits of meat, aided by the warmth of the heating element.

Norman was a very fastidious person and we could never resist playing practical jokes on him. I shudder a bit now when I think of it, but before he, Lois and their children arrived we scattered some peas and onion rings and carrots over the greasy, warm scum in the washing machine. Once our guests had had their soup and were exclaiming how nice it was, we said, 'Oh, we're glad you liked it because we've got enough to last us all winter.'

We then flung open the bifold doors of the alcove to show them the washing machine with the hairy sheep's feet and vegetables floating on the top.

Poor Norman rushed straight off to the toilet and threw up. Afterwards he wouldn't have any more to do with our meal, though Lois was far more understanding – besides, she had the kids to feed, and they sat down and consumed the roast and pudding quite happily.

Our vet school course was pressured and competitive. Knowing that there was a significant failure rate made us all try very hard because after the efforts we had put into gaining a place in the school it was very important not to be in the group that failed. When we were swotting we used to collect 'pearls', pieces of really good information that we would swap and that were supposed to make all the difference between passing and failing.

We told poor Norman that in the horse, and only in the horse, there was another chamber to the heart that pumped blood straight to the brain. Thus the horse was unique in being the only mammal that had a third ventricle. He accepted this pearl with gratitude and traded it for one of his quite legitimate gems – something to do with the pituitary gland, as I recall.

The terrible embarrassment was that Norman actually wrote this in his exam results, and when we told him it had all been a joke he was beside himself with fury, insisting that we go to the lecturer and explain what we'd done so that he wouldn't be unduly penalised.

Tom Scott, of the *Listener* and cartoon fame, began his university career in the vet school with us, and one year he produced the students' revue.

John Gill did his famous monologue as one of the victorious D-Day commanders. Dressed in a gabardine overcoat and a slouch hat, and with the cigarette smoke curling into the lights, he intoned: 'Somewhere, deep in the bowels of the War Office, there had been a ghastly cock-up.'

Tom and I took on the job of doing the little 'fill-in' parts between the scenes when they were fiddling about with the stuff behind the curtain. We had a variety of little numbers worked out, one of which was – it sounds very studentish now – charging across the stage at each other on bicycles and jousting with mops. It all seemed to work pretty well, except that one night, probably the last night, Tom hit me square on the chin with the end of his mop, cutting my chin wide open. Luckily the party started shortly afterwards, so the pain didn't last for long. When I arrived home about three in the morning I looked at this great gash in the mirror and thought, 'I can fix this.'

Hunting around I found my suture material, including a needle holder to hold a tiny needle, and thought, 'Well, I'll just put a couple of stitches in here.'

Holding the wound closed and focusing blearily on the mirror, I positioned the needle and drove it in. Halfway through the pain became excruciating – it was unbelievable that it could be so painful. I had no option but to force it on through and out the other side. I did it – I sewed my chin up, but never will I do it again, and never again will I believe in the anaesthetic effect of alcohol.

Dick Dean had been bitten near the eye when he was young, with the result that his tear duct was blocked and he had a fairly constant stream of tears running down one side of his face. This eye had a slightly different appearance – the corner was slightly scarred and looked as if it were pinched in a little bit.

But Dick was convinced, or at least he convinced me, that this eye had considerable powers, especially over women. He only had to stare at a member of the female sex for a relatively short time and she would start to become compliant with his thoughts.

We were in the library one day and he said, 'I'll show you.' There was a girl sitting about four rows ahead of us, off to one side.

'You watch,' Dick said. He concentrated intently on the girl, who within a short while started to rub her thighs together furiously. This had the effect of drawing her skirt up and Dick said, 'There, I showed you. I told you it worked.'

She didn't go any further, and perhaps it really was a coincidence, but Dick did enjoy considerable success with women. In fact this was one of the few drawbacks of flatting with him. I would be trying to work in my room in the coldest corner of the house while he would be entertaining just through the wall. Mind you, I got better marks than him, but I'm not sure that I wouldn't rather have had a few more Cs.

In the company of the illustrious French sisters Dick and I attended every ball that the university put on, resplendent in our hired dinner suits. For Dick, the money was well invested as he and Janet French were married in our final year.

Part of a veterinary degree involved working on farms during the university vacation. This was to get a basic understanding of how farms worked so that when you did graduate you wouldn't look like a total idiot.

Everybody had to arrange their own positions on farms, which wasn't easy for a town boy, so I had a look in the newspaper's farm pages to see if I could find labouring jobs.

One job I came across looked as if it would suit quite well as it was just out of Christchurch. Steven Minson and his mother and father ran a small mixed dairying and pig farm and wanted a farm labourer for the summer. The thing that annoyed me most about this job was that Steven referred to me as his Man Friday, and judging by the miserable pay I was getting I suppose I was.

He had an amazing method of milking the cows. It was his belief that they would milk best if they entered the cow bale in the same position every day, for every milking. Thus cow number 39 had to be followed by cow number 21 every day, and if a cow chose to get out of position he would race around the crowded yard until he got the right cow and then, belting it mercilessly with a black pipe, would drive it into its right place in the shed. The result was that the shed would be absolutely covered in cow poop and the cows would finally line up in the bale, heaving and panting with their tongues out and their eyes staring, giving hardly any milk at all. I later learnt that this was exactly the wrong thing to do in a milking shed, but Steven was adamant that he knew exactly how to do it all, taking, I expect, special pride in being able to tell this university type exactly where he was going wrong.

About two weeks after I started the job the entire Minson family, mother and father and son, left for a holiday, which was the reason for taking me on in the first place. To look after me they brought in a couple who would take no part in the farming activities but would cook me my meals.

I was still a young, growing boy, and when I came in from feeding the pigs on the first night and sat down the wife handed me a plate of cold meat. I put it down in front of me, added the potatoes, the beetroot and salt and pepper and started tucking in. I looked up and saw them both staring at me. I then realised that the plate they'd given me was to be shared between the three of us. The husband mumbled something like 'If you feed pigs you end up behaving like them.'

The cowshed was more to my liking. I actually developed quite an affinity for the cows and discovered that if you didn't belt the hell out of them they became quite sociable and friendly animals.

While working in the milking shed, true to form, I had a tendency to slip into a dream state in which I would act out my little fantasies. Of course the high-powered hose used for cleaning the yard was an ideal fantasy tool, and it was difficult when Steven returned from holiday to explain to him why his radio didn't work. I couldn't quite bring myself to tell him that I'd hosed it completely off the wall during my fire-fighting fantasy.

My other job was with the Judge family, who farmed near Culverden. This set-up seemed straight out of feudal England. We would line up in the morning to be told our job for the day, and that was the last we'd see of the boss. When you looked along the row of workers they formed a funny motley little crew. There was a tractor driver who'd been employed there since he was a boy. He suffered from a chronic sinus problem and had no handkerchief, so breakfast was something to be avoided as he would invariably sneeze all over the table.

The cook, like many cooks, was an inveterate alcoholic and so meals were either burnt or non-existent. He was assisted in his recreational duties by the shepherd. The last member was the son-in-law, who was less welcomed by the owners of the property than any of the hired labour.

As I was a vet student I was given the job – and I enjoyed it – of looking after the injured horses, of which there seemed to be quite a few. Horses and I have always had a strange sort of relationship. The Judges' horses were mostly valuable thoroughbreds. One, I recall, had gone through the lid of a well and ripped all the skin up its leg, and it was my job to change the dressing on the wound every day. The wound was always sore, the horse understandably always flighty, and I was very nervous, so the results were fairly unpredictable.

The first day I treated it I tied the horse to a rail and began working on the dressing. Of course as soon as it felt the pain the horse pulled back and the rail flew loose. Next thing a 12-foot beam was whirling around the horse's head, hitting me or the horse or both of us each time it swung around. Every time it hit the horse it would gallop another three laps around the yard, and it wasn't until the owner came back that we were able to get things back under control.

Neither the Judges nor I were too unhappy when my vacation came to an end.

5

Back to the West Coast

It came as quite a surprise to me that I was a very good student once my enthusiasm was aroused. In all the years at Massey I didn't fail a single subject and several times passed with an A. At last I was a fully-qualified vet. There were plenty of job vacancies on the notice board, but I knew where I was going. Hokitika and its social life beckoned and I was determined to answer the call.

After the fiasco of Mr Reilly's cow with cancer eye I was nervous at the thought of venturing into South Westland again. The entire community of Fox Glacier had very quickly learned of my misadventure, so they were feeling pretty nervous too. In fact, if I was on duty and somebody phoned from that part of the world they would hear my voice and ask, 'Oh, is Vince about?' or 'Is there any other vet there?'

In my own defence, I have to say that I operated on another cow with a cancer eye some time later, using local anaesthetic only. This cow also died, but I was a bit wiser by then and insisted on doing a post mortem. The tumour had actually spread to the lungs, which I suspect was what had happened to the first cow. But I was too new and embarrassed then to insist on a post mortem.

One weekend I was the vet on duty for the entire coast, from Reefton through to Fox Glacier. When John Sullivan from Fox Glacier rang up to say he needed a vet down there he went through the usual routine.

'Who's on duty?'

'Me. David Marshall.'

A long pause.

'No one else on duty at all?'

'No,' I said.

Another long pause.

'What about the vet from Reefton? Is he about?'

'Sorry, mate. Only me.'

So this was how seriously they viewed the possibility of having me arrive down there.

'Well, all right. You might as well come down. The bull's got a broken jaw, but I really only need an insurance certificate. You are licensed to do that, aren't you?' he asked suspiciously.

I drove down and we had a look at the jaw. As John had suspected, it was broken; with the bull's head in the crush I could feel the gap in the bone and when I looked in his mouth I could see the step down in the line of the lower molars. Here, I thought to myself, was my chance to redeem myself in the eyes of the locals.

I started talking enthusiastically about putting steel plates in the jaw in an attempt to save the beast, and initially John also became quite enthusiastic.

'Yes, good,' he said. 'Okay, let's do it.'

So we let the bull out and went back for a cup of tea.

'We'll need an X-ray,' I said. 'And some lights would be useful.'

'Well, of course you know that means we'll need to get the power. The only place you can hold that bull is in the yards – you can't have him anywhere else – and that's about half a mile from the nearest source of electricity. Much as I'd like to see you succeed, David, and as much as I think you're capable of succeeding, I think we've got to give in.'

Noticing my disappointment, John tried to console me. 'Don't worry. I've got him well insured. You can shoot him, if you like.'

He got out his little Fergie tractor with a sheep crate on the back, put me in it, and handed me a single-shot .22.

'Okay,' he said. 'Here's what we'll do. We'll just drive up beside him and when we get close you just let rip.'

'Okay,' I muttered, not feeling very confident at all.

We drove out into the paddock, which looked more like a re-stored river bed, almost as though it had been border-dyked in every direction. There were channels and ridges everywhere; it was so bumpy that I had to hang on to the crate for dear life as we drove off towards the bull. When we'd got to within about 50 yards of him the bull started to trot off. John sped up a little, and so did the bull. The bull and the tractor were still about 50 yards apart, but now travelling at over 15 kilometres an hour.

John turned around on the seat and shouted, 'Just shoot him whenever you're ready.'

'Oh well,' I thought, 'my reputation was never much in Fox Glacier so I probably can't make it any worse.' I pointed vaguely at the lumbering animal and pulled the trigger. The bull dropped stone dead. John whipped around again, stared sharply at me for a long moment and said, 'Make sure that gun's unloaded before you go waving it about any more.'

After that people started ringing up and saying, 'Can we have David Marshall come and have a look at this cow (or bull or what-ever)? We only want to see him.'

Fox Glacier became more or less a second home for me. I became the unofficial Fox Glacier vet, based mostly on the fact that by sheer good luck I had shot dead a bull from the back of a bouncing tractor.

When I first arrived in Hokitika the secretary of the vet club put me up in the Pioneer Hotel. Hokitika still has about a dozen of these classic old pubs, which are usually wooden, two-storeyed, owned by a husband and wife, open all hours, nice and cheap, with great food and always a great place to stay. The Pioneer's bedrooms all had windows looking out onto the footpath. The first night I stayed there I forgot to close my window, and when I woke in the morning there were about six of the local girls with their heads in the window, checking to see what the new vet was like.

The new vet didn't feel too good, actually. He'd been in the bar the night before and probably looked a bit ashen as well as a bit pimply. I don't think I was seen as the catch of the year. But Mr and Mrs Gardener thought I was great. I was allowed to have breakfast in the kitchen, and they cooked up meals for me at any time of the day or night.

The bars in these pubs were magic. You put your money on the bar when you went in and every time you went up for a drink the barman just took the money out of your pile and put the change back. He had a far better idea of counting out change than I did, especially as the night wore on. But the thing that really impressed me was that if you left the pub – and often we went to more than one pub – the barman would put your change in a glass with your name on it and place it up on the shelf. You might not arrive back for about three or four weeks, but when you did they would bring down this glass and say, 'Oh, here's your change from when you were here last time.' So you can talk about the café society of Paris or Auckland or even Christchurch, but nothing could ever measure up to the pub society of Hokitika.

Hokitika had a famous pie cart – Bill Sadler's pie cart – often the last place at night that people visited after the pub scene. Bill had a bit of a problem with drinking, as did a lot of people in Hokitika, and he would keep whisky in a Worcester sauce bottle so that his wife, who was quite a domineering, strong-minded sort of a person, wouldn't notice him quietly swigging away. His other foible was to turn on the tap to fill the Zip in the pie cart and forget about it, so the water would steadily mount up the glass tube until it hit the whistle and spray the entire clientele of the pie cart with hot water.

Some nights when Mrs Sadler wasn't on duty Bill would take a break and go down to the Southland Hotel, which was just down the road. We also used to spend the interval at the Southland during a play I was performing in – as a single male with an interest in drama I found myself quickly in demand. We happened to be already propping up the bar there one night when Bill turned up. The whole cast of the play were there, and I was wearing a kilt for the part I played. When Bill saw me he extended his jaw, held his nose and started hitting his throat with the side of his hand to imitate the sound of the bagpipes. But it was getting late for Bill, in years as well as in the hour of the day, and he was a bit forceful with his hand against his throat, with the result that he knocked himself clean out. Amazingly enough, the locals just dragged old Bill out, left him in the foyer and carried on. About an hour later Bill staggered out and went back to the pie cart, apparently none the worse for wear.

The West Coast, perhaps because of its isolation, seems to attract unusual people and many of them, either through loneliness or gregariousness, end up in the pub. Digger was a seaman who had retired from the sea to live on the West Coast. He had been a serious alcoholic at one time, but by the time I met him he was strictly a serious tea drinker.

'Y'know,' he said once, 'sometimes I used to get so far out of it, I could see myself coming back.'

Digger still enjoyed the atmosphere of a pub and was happy to sit for hours sipping tea with his dog asleep under the leaner. He would bring his own teabags and the publican gave him the hot water free. He was at various times an eel fisherman and a possum trapper, and was adamant that he never had or would accept a government hand-out. But times were so bad for Digger that occasionally he was forced to eat the possums.

'How do you catch your possums, Digger?' I asked once.

'Oh, we kill them with cyanide.'

'Well, there'd be a fair chance you'd have poisoned yourself, wouldn't there?' I ventured.

This thought took him by surprise. 'I always gut them first. What do you think would be the symptoms?

'Breathlessness, I suppose.'

'Oh, yeah,' he said. 'I've had that quite often.'

Lyall Daley was a house surgeon at Hokitika Hospital who was interested in animals and beer, which is why we met at the pub. One day he was moaning that the hospital was too small and there was no opportunity to develop any surgical skills, so I suggested he come out with me on my calls one day. If there were any operations he could do them.

About a week later the opportunity did arise. A local farmer had a calf with an umbilical hernia, quite a big one. Normally such hernias don't need operating on, but this one was so big it might have caused trouble later. So I gathered Lyall, the bucket, the disinfectant and the instruments and we assembled on the farm. My dog Kelly was in attendance as usual.

The plan was that I would give the anaesthetic while Lyall did the surgery. Everything was ready, with the bucketful of instruments sterilised with disinfectant. The farmer and his wife brought the calf out and held on to it while I gave it some Pentothal in the jugular vein. It staggered about three steps and fell down onto some rotten logs.

'Good,' I thought, 'that seems to be working well.'

But the calf had landed on a wasps' nest. The number of wasps that flew out of that small hole in the ground underneath those logs was unbelievable. The farmer and his wife both disappeared with astonishing speed into the house at the top of the hill. Most of the wasps focused on Kelly, who began running around with about a hundred of the beasts attached to her. I picked her up and dumped her in the bucket of disinfectant, which killed the wasps but probably de-sterilised the instruments. Then we dragged the calf off the heap.

The wasps by this time had transferred their attentions to Lyall and me. Finally we pulled the calf far enough away from the wasps' nest to allow them to return to it without any further distraction, and only then were we able to top up the anaesthetic, give the instruments a bit more disinfectant and have Lyall perform the surgery.

It was all very uneventful, except that I had to tell Lyall how to do everything. At the end, when we had packed up, gathered everything together and set off in the car, Lyall said to me, 'And how many of those have you done?'

I said, 'That was the first one.'

Lyall went on to become a specialist and he wrote me a note some years later reminding me of the beginnings of his surgical career.

I'd known Mr Waters for several months before I realised he was the stores foreman at Hokitika Hospital. The times I'd met him in the pub we'd usually talked about fishing or rugby, so when one day he invited me to come and look over his storeroom to see if there was anything that we wanted for the vet clinic, I was overjoyed and couldn't get there quickly enough.

I've always been a keen fossicker and collector, since my early days in Urlwin's dump. Mr Waters could sense my appreciation and enjoyment and he was very generous. He kept saying, 'That'll probably go to Corso anyway, so you might as well have it.'

He gave me a big box and we went around the shelves of the storeroom gathering up catheters and drapes and gloves and syringes. But the treasure, the joy of my life, was an ECG machine, which must have been one of the early models. It had brass hinges and came in a beautiful mahogany box, with ivory labels and inscribed black lettering. It was a magnificent instrument.

To have an ECG was potentially a real boon for me and I set about learning to use it. I've always been guilty of over-enthusiasm, extolling the virtues of the latest gadget I've got and telling everybody what it can do before I've taught myself how to use it adequately. I always know what *it* can do, but I should be more specific about what *I* can do.

Well, I came unstuck with this ECG machine. The very first animal I tried it out on was a trotter named Red Baron, which was owned by a publican in Westport. Red Baron was a roarer, which meant that part of his voice box was paralysed. Each time he breathed in his floppy, paralysed vocal cord was sucked into his windpipe, making a roaring noise and interfering with the flow of air, which is of course quite critical for a racehorse.

The experts, including Professor Goulden from the vet school – my old lecturer – said that these horses had a heart problem that could only be seen on an ECG machine, so it was important that before doing surgery or even anaesthetising them, an ECG was done.

I now had the perfect piece of equipment for the job so off I went to Westport, all ready to do an operation I'd never done before with an ECG I'd never used before. It was raining when I arrived so the horse had been boxed in the trainer's dry garage, near the power. We stood Red Baron on a rubber mat to provide insulation, as described in the book. I had no proper electrodes to attach to the horse's legs so I used syringe needles, driven into the muscles of each leg with the wires twisted around them. It seems pretty barbaric nowadays, but it worked pretty well then. Luckily he was a very placid beast. Next came the extension cord from the house carrying the power. This was plugged into the ECG machine and everyone crowded in to watch.

I leaned forward and flicked the switch.

The needle seemed to be a bit erratic, so I changed the setting on one of the knobs and was immediately seized by an amazingly powerful electric shock, which threw me to the ground. My hand remained clamped onto the knob so tightly that I was unable to release myself from the machine and lay there convulsing with the power of the electric shock. The horse's owners, thankfully, thought to turn the machine off, so eventually I recovered. But I decided there and then that the ECG would have to remain a museum relic.

Race meetings on the West Coast were always an important part of the region's life and, as I have described, the vet assumed increased importance on this day. He had to examine horses that the stipendiary steward felt didn't run fast enough, or ran too fast. He also had to swab horses. This was something quite new to me as a townie. A pair of tongs holding a swab soaked in acetic acid was pushed into the horse's mouth and around the tongue before being forced between the teeth for the horse to chew on. This caused profuse salivation, which was caught in a stainless steel pot to become Sample A.

The second sample was much more difficult, as it involved a urine collection. Theoretically horses will urinate after they've been hosed down and are cooling off. Many horses are, however, unaware of this fact. Quite often an hour would go past and the horse had still failed to urinate. There were many tricks to encourage them, such as kicking the straw up underneath the horse's belly, turning on all the taps, or tuneless and continuous whistling. Quite often these tricks worked better on the vet than they did on the horse.

So for the poor vet it wasn't really a social day, spending, as he did, most of it hiding in a barn out at the back of the race track. Occasionally, though, an emergency would alter the whole colour of the day. This is what happened at the Westport races.

The call on the loud-speaker, 'Would the vet please come to the secretary's office' always produced in me a certain clenching of the vitals. There was always drama to follow.

On this occasion I arrived to find two very anxious men in their sports coats and ties, the connections of the racehorse. (Connections can mean anything from trainer to owner through to the boy who cleans out the boxes.)

It transpired that the horse to which they were connected had been brought all the way up from Wingatui in Southland, so they were obviously expecting it to win. During the morning it had been left unattended and had chewed a big chunk off the wooden railing of its yard. Horses that do this are usually called wind-suckers, or crib-biters. They set their teeth against the rail and bite against it to allow themselves to swallow air – a habit usually brought on by boredom. Often when they do this they clench down hard enough to take a piece of wood off the rail, which is what this horse had done. It had attempted to swallow the wood, which was now stuck in the back of its throat.

The horse was quite distressed, dribbling watery saliva from its nose, and coughing and retching.

'This horse has to race in half an hour,' one of the handlers said. 'What are you going to do?'

They don't teach you this sort of stuff at vet school. The back of a horse's throat is no place for the human hand so, in desperation, I decided that the only thing I could do was to push my stomach tube down its throat and try to push the piece of wood into its stomach.

A stomach tube is usually passed down the nose and swallowed by the horse so it goes into the oesophagus. In my anxiety – or maybe it was the horse's distress – the tube went down the windpipe. On this occasion it was an absolute godsend, for the tube irritated the horse so much that it gave a mighty cough. Up came the piece of wood and the horse was cured.

'Oh, great work!' said the owner, pushing money into my hand. 'You're an absolute genius.'

I swelled up visibly and walked off to put the money straight on the tote. The horse came dead last.

The Warwick brothers had a farm in Mahinapua, not far from the pub. They also had a run-off up the Mikinui Gorge. For most farmers the run-off was where you put dry stock, but for the Warwick brothers it was strictly reserved for shooting deer, and they were addicted to shooting deer. In fact they were quite a hard-bitten bunch all over.

Rumour had it that the father, as a young man, came home from the pub one night and was unfortunate enough to be peeing out the window when the sash cord broke. The heavy window fell and crushed his penis. There was a happy ending to the story though. Apparently, the nurse who attended him fell in love with him as he recovered in hospital. Against all odds, the Warwick brothers were the result of the subsequent marriage.

They were rebellious, difficult and hopeless farmers. Calls to visit their farm were always received with some trepidation, and this call, when they said they had a cow down, turned out to be no different.

Dairy farms are laid out with a central race and paddocks on either side. We walked down the race past three paddocks. No gravel had been laid so it was too muddy to allow a vehicle down. In one of the paddocks, just near the gate, a cow was down, lying on her side. She had started to bloat and looked quite distressed.

'Couldn't you have propped her up and made her comfortable?' I said angrily.

When I examined her I discovered she had a broken leg. 'She's probably caught it in this bloody swamp you're pleased to call a race.' I lost my temper. 'If you did more farming and less deer-stalking your cows would do much better. We'll have to put this cow down.'

'Okay,' said the younger brother, 'I'll go and get the gun,' and he wandered back up the lane. After my outburst the older brother moved some distance from me, without speaking. Suddenly the cow, which was between us, groaned and slumped down dead. I turned round, and there up at the house was the younger brother with his rifle steadied against the open window frame. He had shot the cow, lying within six feet of me, from fully 350 yards.

Smiling crookedly, the older brother wagged his finger at me and said, 'Don't forget, this is Stan Graham country!'

I was in Franz Joseph one afternoon doing a pregnancy test on a mare. This involves inserting a lubricated, gloved hand into the mare's rectum and feeling for the pregnant uterus through the wall of the bowel. In the next door paddock the farmer was on his tractor feeding out his cattle. He climbed off when he saw me, jumped over the fence and came over to me.

'Are you the vet?' he asked, which surprised me rather, standing as I was with my hand up a horse's rectum. When I nodded he asked me if I would come and see his brother's cow.

'That's fine,' I replied. 'That'll be no trouble at all.'

'Great,' he said. 'My brother works in the sawmill. He doesn't finish work till about five o'clock, so if that's still okay we'll meet you in the Franz Josef pub straight after that.'

So five o'clock came and I drove down to the Franz Joseph pub, which is quite smart by West Coast standards – lots of marble and stone. I went into the bar and, mindful of the fact that I was still working, ordered a small three-ounce 'pony beer', as it was called in those days. The bar was almost empty, so I sat on this thimble of beer and sipped away at it until, at about six o'clock, the guy off the tractor turned up, which cheered me up because I didn't really know anybody there.

'Oh good, I'm glad you're here,' he said. 'I told my brother and he'll be here as soon as he can. You having a beer?'

'Just a pony.'

'Righty oh then, let's have a game of pool.'

So he put our names up on the board, and we had a game and won. This hotel, like most on the Coast, decrees that King of the Table applies. In other words, if you win the challenger puts the fifty cents in the slot on the table to pay for the next game and the loser in each game shouts a jug of beer. So we carefully drank some of that, and next thing the challengers were saying, 'Okay, you guys, mugs away!' meaning that they wanted to start a new game.

'Yeah, youse guys break!'

We won that one as well and another jug of beer appeared.

'When's your brother coming?' I asked my partner. 'You know, I've really got to get back. It's a fair drive to Hokitika tonight.'

'Well, I've told him. He'll be here as soon as he can.'

So we had another game of pool and another jug of beer. In the end I lost count of how many games we'd won. At about a quarter to ten the owner of the sick cow appeared. I was feeling a bit pippy by then. I thought this was no good at all and said as much.

'Hang on, mate. Me brother's been lookin' after you pretty all right, hasn't he?' he replied. 'How many jugs have you had? And you haven't had to pay for any of them!'

'Okay, okay,' I said, omitting to point out that my pool-playing skills were the reason for the free beer. 'Can we go and have a look at your cow now?'

'Hang on a minute, mate,' he said, 'I've only just got here.' So he had a jug of beer.

They finally kicked us out about a quarter to 11. I stood in the carpark in a steady drizzle, feeling quite depressed. 'It's getting pretty bloody late, you know. It's going to take me all my time to get back to Hoki tonight as it is and it's pitch dark. Do you reckon she'll hang on till I'm down this way again?' I was starting to worry about falling asleep on the way home.

'Now listen here,' the cow's owner threatened, the beer starting to make him belligerent. 'The last time I seen her she was flat on her side with her belly as tight as a drum and her back leg sticking in the air.'

Probably dead by now then, I thought gloomily.

He gathered momentum. 'Besides, you're only down here once in a blue moon and then you'll want to charge extra mileage!'

'Oh well,' I said wearily, 'come on, we'd better go and have a look at your cow.'

So I started to dig around in the boot of the car, thinking about what we might need, because we were going to go in his ute.

'What d'you think's wrong with it?' I asked.

'I don't know. You're the bloody vet.'

So I took stuff to cover every contingency in a big bag that we put in the back of his ute. I slumped in the passenger seat while he did up the binder twine holding the door shut, and off we went.

'Where is this cow?' I asked.

'It's in the run-off,' he said.

My heart sank even further. The run-off on the West Coast means that it's on the other side of the river, there's no bridge, there'll be no yards, and there probably won't be any fences.

All three factors applied in this case. We pulled up on the river bank with the headlights shining out across the water. He put a miner's light on his head, powered with a motorbike battery tied to his belt with binder twine, and we waded the river, with me stumbling under the weight of a large bag of drugs and instruments.

As we started off across the paddocks my arms began to feel painfully stretched. 'How far do you think this'll be?'

'Well, last time I saw her she was just over the other side of that little hill,' he said, pointing to a large black shape in the moonlight, virtually on the horizon. I staggered along behind him for about a kilometre across a swampy paddock broken by tussocks, rushes and small streams. Just before we reached the brow of the hill he stopped and knelt down.

'Okay, here's the plan of attack,' he said, his voice reduced to a whisper. 'She's pretty knackered so I don't think she'll kick up much of a fuss if I go over the top of the hill, grab her by the tail and hold her so you can have a decent look at her.'

He steadied himself briefly, then brandishing his arm in a gesture that only Geronimo would fully comprehend, launched himself over the top. The light blazing from his helmet lit up parts of the low cloud above us as he advanced upward – I've always thought that Coasters have a natural sense of the dramatic.

When I arrived over the top I could tell immediately that this cow wasn't as sick as he thought she was. She probably thought she was being run down by a train. He'd got her by the tail all right, but all I could see was his light disappearing down the hill in huge great arcing leaps. He seemed to be shouting my name as he went. The light continued down the hill in great bounds for quite a distance before teetering around for a bit in little dancing dots and then suddenly going out. He'd gone into the swamp.

So I sat down and had a smoke. After a while I could hear a wheezing asthmatic noise and the squelching of his boots as he emerged from the swamp and started up the hill. The cloud started to clear and soon I could see him in the moonlight. His helmet and battery had disappeared, the light was hanging around his neck, and he was covered in mud and duck weed.

Finally he was standing in front of me. I looked up at him as he spoke.

'Well, what do you think's wrong with her?'

After-hours calls in Hokitika were always a bit fraught. There was always driving involved, there were often large, dangerous animals at the end of the journey, and usually the vet was sorely ill-equipped.

Ten o'clock on Saturday night was not a good time to find a vet in Hokitika, but I happened to be home when the phone rang.

'Gidday, it's Harry Grocott here, from Whataroa. The girl on the exchange said your car was up your drive, so I thought I'd catch you at home. I want you to come down and have a look at a horse of mine, tonight if you can. She's got colic pretty bad, been up and down all day. The way she's going, she'll find herself dead in the morning. Besides, she's my best cutting horse and you hate to see them in pain, don't you, especially when they cost so much.'

He waited expectantly, hoping he had pushed all my emotional buttons.

'Okay, okay,' I said. 'Put a cover on her and keep her warm and walking. I'll be down as fast as I can.'

Colic is a high-risk condition. The usual treatment is to give an injection of a smooth muscle relaxant, which reduces the spasming contractions of the gut. If the cause is functional, such as a severe inflammation, the horse will respond. If it is a mechanical obstruction the horse will die. It is possible to operate, but the success rate is poor. But I decided that if I had to drive all the way to Whataroa, which is about two hours away from Hokitika, I needed to be prepared for everything, so I went down to the clinic and sterilised all the equipment necessary to do an abdominal operation on a horse.

I took a dozen bottles of Pentothal and my flatmate, who was the local baker, Bernie Preston. Bernie had no special skills as an anaesthetist, but he was a sensible person.

'There's nothing to these anaesthetics, really, Bernie. I'll get him knocked out and once we start operating you can take over.'

An image of Superman jumping off the coalshed roof surfaced from my subconscious. I quickly suppressed it and went on. 'As the horse starts to wake up, his eyes will wobble back and forwards – it's called nystagmus. That's your cue to give him another 10ml of Pentothal. I've brought a catheter that I scored from the hospital. I'll stick it in his jugular vein and you can just connect the syringe to it each time you want give him some more.'

'I don't know about this,' said Bernie. 'What if the horse dies? Harry Grocott knows my father pretty well, you see.'

'If it dies, it won't be your fault. If we do nothing, it'll probably die anyway. Tell you what, if it lives I'll get Harry to shout you a crate of beer.'

Bernie relaxed a bit after that and settled himself more comfortably in the passenger seat to enjoy the drive. When we pulled up at the farm Harry and the farm manager from the Lands and Survey block down the road had the horse walking around the back lawn.

'She's got pretty bloody cold while we've been waiting for you. I've had to put the eiderdown off our bed under her cover. The missus is over the hill for the weekend but I don't s'pose she'll mind.'

Harry's wife's inclination to throw things was widely reported on the Coast, so this suggested the horse was quite important to him.

The diagnosis of abdominal accidents in horses is not an easy subject, and I have to admit that I was no expert at it. But I felt confident as I put the thermometer up the horse's anus. The temperature was normal, but the end of the thermometer was covered in blood. With hindsight I realise there are many conditions, not requiring surgery, that could have produced this blood, but I decided that this horse had to be opened up instantly or it was going to die. I didn't actually say so, but I thought that it was probably going to die anyway.

So we gave the horse a dose of Pentothal and once it was asleep I handed over the anaesthetic reins to Bernie, who sat himself down at the head end of the horse to watch the eyes and give another 10ml every now and then. We laid the horse on its back on the back lawn and, with an extension cord leading out from the house, hung a light bulb from the clothesline immediately over the horse's abdomen. I started to shave the horse's belly.

'Now, we need a surgical drape. You haven't got an old sheet, have you?'

Harry flinched. 'No,' he said slowly. 'Not an old one, but hang on.'

He ran inside. The light in his bedroom was turned on briefly and he re-emerged, carrying a double sheet. 'I don't suppose she'll mind under the circumstances,' he muttered.

I dipped the sheet in a bucket of disinfectant, tore a gap through the middle of it and spread it on the horse's belly with the tear over the part I intended to cut. With the surgical preparation done I made a huge incision from breast bone to pelvis to get good exposure.

... about a million moths turned up, attracted by the light.

Shortly after that about a million moths turned up, attracted by the light, and they all fell into the wound. Initially I fastidiously removed every moth as it fell in, but it soon became impossible to keep up with them. Another subconscious urge made me notice that my gum-boots still did not conform to my skinny calves as I plunged my scrubbed-up hands into this seething cauldron of intestines.

Horses have an enormous amount of guts. I started feeling around inside, not quite sure what I was going to find. Just as my elbow sank from view my hand came upon a hard ball. This must be the kidney, I thought, and drew it up into the wound to see if I could identify it. As I got it closer to the incision it began to flip around a large segment of intestine to which it appeared to be attached by quite a long stalk, like a Maori poi. Somehow this mass had managed to twist itself around the intestine and strangulate it.

'I think I've found the problem, Harry!' I shouted. Soon after the moths had starting falling in he had decided he needed to go inside to look for something. 'I think we're onto a winner here.'

It was a very easy job to put some clamps on the stalk, tie it off and just cut the lump off. The problem came when we tried to put all the guts back in. The gas in the intestine must have swelled all the organs so that the edge of the wound wouldn't do up. It was like someone who'd put on weight since the last time they had put their suit on. I started to get a bit desperate. The heavy catgut, which is the usual material to sew up the innermost layer of such a wound, would break just as I started to get the edges of the wound to touch each other. The more times I failed the more the guts seemed to bulge.

'How much longer do you think you'll be, Davey? I've only got a bottle and a half left.'

I had almost forgotten about Bernie.

'What'll happen if the horse wakes up before you can get that hole sewn up?' I had another momentary image, as I glanced over my shoulder, of an army blanket hanging limply down my back.

I said to the farm manager, 'Do you think you can scrub your hands up and help me?'

He washed his hands briefly in the disinfectant and plunged them into the abdomen. He nodded his head in the direction of the house and Harry. 'This stuff doesn't worry me. I was on the chain in the freezing works for a few years.'

The frayed, oily cuffs of his overalls trailed behind his typical farmer's fingers, great thick knotted cords, deeply ingrained with grime and bacteria, as they squeezed and groped through the guts.

'Nice and warm, aren't they?'

We struggled on, breaking stitch after stitch, until he said, 'Why don't you get a big needle and some binder twine?'

'You can't leave those sort of stitches in the wound.'

'No, no,' he said. 'Do about half a dozen of them, put in millions of your little stitches, then cut the binder twine out and see if your little stitches hold.'

'All right.' I did exactly what the farmer suggested. I put in some big stitches with some binder twine that had been dunked in the ubiquitous bucket of disinfectant, and the edges came together quite nicely. Then followed about a hundred catgut stitches holding the edges of the wound together, followed by another row of stitches pulling the fat layer together. I carefully cut the binder twine stitches and removed them. Everything seemed to hold, so I started on the skin layer.

At about three in the morning the operation was finished. The horse had had 11 5ml bottles of Pentothal and was still perfectly asleep.

'Glad I could be of some help,' said the farm manager, admiring his bloody fingers. I've always thought I'd make a good vet!'

As we were leaving, Harry reappeared. 'Thanks, men. I'd put you up for the night but I'm a bit short of bedclothes.'

Miserable old bastard, I thought, but I was actually quite pleased to leave. I had visions of his horse breaking all its stitches as it got up in the morning, tripping up on its guts as it careered across the paddock and dying an awful death. I didn't really want to be around when it woke up.

I didn't hear anything more from the owner for a long time, so I decided to send the bill. I charged about $100, which I thought was remarkably fair. It didn't take long for him to respond.

'Harry Grocott here,' he said, breathing heavily down the phone. 'I'm not happy about that bill you sent. It's cost me a new sheet and an eiderdown and the missus has busted half the crockery in the house over me head. And the power bill's shot out of all proportion, what with the light being on all night.'

'Hang on,' I interrupted. 'You can't blame me for the time the operation took.'

'Yes I can,' he said. 'If you'd brought decent sewing-up string you could have been done in half the time and I wouldn't have had to give your mate a dozen beer for helping.'

'Well, at least you've got a live horse out of it,' I replied, feeling a bit defeated.

'Yeah, that's the other thing I wanted to talk about. I don't know what you and that baker did when I was inside, but no one's been able to catch the horse since.'

When I sent the sample to the lab they were so impressed with the success of the surgery that they wrote it up in their laboratory newsletter. I spoke to one of the horse lecturers at the vet school some time afterwards, and he described having done the same thing with every ancillary help that the vet school had available, and the horse died.

Which just goes to show that West Coast horses are tough!

6

More Wild West
Adventures

One of the social highlights of the Hokitika year was the ball at the mental asylum on top of the hill. The superintendent was renowned for his ability to provide marvellous hospitality, even by West Coast standards, so everybody clamoured to go. The vets and the doctors of the area felt themselves to be kindred spirits – perhaps they all felt equally threatened by the remoteness of the place – so the vets were all invited to go to the ball. I had hired a dinner suit and my partner looked absolutely gorgeous in a black evening dress. We were just about to leave when the phone rang and a farmer from Tirawati, which is halfway between Otira and Kumara, rang to say that his horse had cut its leg badly.

'I'll do it quickly and we can still make it to the ball,' I told my partner cheerfully.

The drive to Tirawati was conducted in stony silence.

We found the horse and its owners waiting for us in a large shed. Because I had left without checking through the boot I found when I arrived that I didn't have the right gear to perform a general anaesthetic on a horse. The horse, a yearling, was too difficult to stitch up with just a twitch and a local anaesthetic, but rather than give up I returned to the car to have another rummage through the boot, aware of the glares that Robyn directed at me every time she caught my eye.

I found a bottle of Rompun, a new drug intended for cattle, which had been very successful. The technique in cattle was to give the injection of Rompun first and then to pull the beast to the ground, using a series of three half hitches around the neck, around the chest behind the elbows, with a final half hitch in front of the thighs. I felt sure that this technique would work in a horse, so I gave it the Rompun, attached the rope, and said to everybody present, 'Okay, come and swing on this rope.'

Everybody, including Robyn, came to my assistance, but instead of sinking gracefully to the ground, the horse rose majestically in the air. In a corner of the shed was a pile of furniture – tables, chairs, bookcases and cupboards, all stacked up together. The horse climbed the entire stack of furniture, kicked it to bits and disappeared into the night, dragging my good rope with it.

We had a quick look for the horse, but it had disappeared into the bush behind the house.

The farmer said, 'Well, never mind. When she comes back I'll give you a call and we can still do the job.'

So off we went to the ball, with me thinking about my good rope having gone missing and feeling a little shame-faced about the results of my lateral thinking. I'm not sure what my partner was thinking but she seemed rather quiet.

Three days later the owner rang up to say that the filly had come back out of the bush and the rope was gone. Would I like to come and sew the leg up? This time I was properly prepared. Under a general anaesthetic it was quite easy to clean up the wound, which had become infected, place the sutures, and give some antibiotics.

I saw him about a month later and enquired after the filly.

'Oh, marvellous result there,' he said. 'You know, after about a week, the stitches came out and pus flowed freely from the wound. Then this lovely healthy knob of proud flesh grew and now it's healed like a charm.'

This was not the way I had expected the wound to heal at all, but he went on to say – and I never was sure whether this was with heavy irony or not – 'Neil Bruere couldn't have done better.'

Neil Bruere is one of New Zealand's foremost vets, who began his career on the West Coast and finished it as an Emeritus Professor at Massey University.

Right from the beginning the farmers of the West Coast were marvellously hospitable and friendly to me. Many newcomers feel that unless they have been a Coaster for three generations or more the locals will still consider them as outsiders, but I found that to be quite untrue. Perhaps being a vet gave me a bit more social standing, but it was always clear that I was more than welcome. I would often arrive back at the clinic after a day's work, having eaten about 30 or 40 peanut brownies and drunk so many cups of tea that my stomach would splash as I got out of the car.

I loved the driving between farms. There was an area by Lake Ianthe that I found particularly fascinating. The bush had been milled and then burned off, and it was best seen early in the morning, when there was almost always a grey mist coming from the lake. Through the watercolour wash and the vague yellow-green colour of the grass protruded the blackened stumps of the old totaras, matais and white pines. It was so eerie and primordial that I could almost imagine seeing moas prancing about by the lake.

Jack Delaney lived in this area, right on the shores of Lake Ianthe.

Apparently he had been left at the altar as a young man and had never quite recovered. There were eight gates between the main road and his house – he was not a man who went to town very often.

There was a lost-generation mood about Jack's place. As I went down the drive lined with split totara fence posts covered in green-grey lichen, the mood of neglect and despondency would settle around me. Through the yard, over in the distance, was a pile of timber. This was Jack's house. The area had been milled in the 1920s, and Jack had collected all the off-cuts and slabs and piled them against his house. The windows were completely obscured and the only gap in the timber was where the door opened. The timber slabs had been there for so long that lichen had grown all over them.

Old Jack appeared through the gap, looking much the same colour as his surroundings. He wore an ancient sports coat, probably green when new, but now bleached by rain and sun. His hair would have been white had it been clean; his bushy eyebrows, which met in the middle and almost obscured his eyes, were grey-black and his beard – he wouldn't have called it a beard, it was more as if he just hadn't shaved for a while – was grey with a touch of ginger in it. A few red-brown areas of rusty corrugated iron on the roof of the cow-shed were the only colours to clash with the all-pervading pastels.

'Come in, come in,' Jack said. 'I've got something I want to show you inside.'

Jack's voice always caught me surprise. It seemed to be about three sizes too small for him. It took quite a while for my eyes to accustom to the gloom so I could read the labels on the bottles of pills that Jack had offered me.

'Now look at these,' he said. 'I want to check. I've been to that doctor in Hokitika again recently and they've changed my pills. I want you to look and tell me whether you think they'll do the job.'

Jack suffered from heart problems and every time I visited him he asked me the same question, and every time I said, 'No, they'll be fine, Jack.' He was greatly reassured and felt much more confident about the pills after the vet had okayed them.

Jack's scepticism about doctors was said to be well founded. Several years previously he had been operated on and found to have advanced cancer, so he was closed up and sent home to die. But dying was not on Jack's agenda, and he was still angrily living on seven or eight years later.

'How about a glass of beer and a bit of bread before we get on with the job?' he said.

I refused quickly. I knew about Jack's bread. Apparently he would get up in the morning and mix his dough on a tray before taking the whole lot back to bed with him. He would lie there for two or three hours, cuddling the dough under the blankets until it rose. Then he would put the mixture into a cold wood oven, light the oven, then leave the bread for a few hours to bake.

The result might have been all right when it was fresh, but it was never fresh. The only time I was ever foolish enough to accept Jack's offer he used a tomahawk to chip a piece off for me to eat. The beer was even worse. He bought it from a hotel, but because he was mostly on his own he would have one glass and then put a cork in the bottle. If the beer wasn't visibly mouldy he would consider it fit to drink. So I was quite happy to escape the house and get on with the job.

Jack's passion was his Jersey cows. I can understand that, for I too think Jersey cows are lovely. They have soft, gentle faces and they smell warm and grassy. At the time I arrived the Coast was enjoying a surge of prosperity, so herringbone sheds were the norm, or even the odd rotary cowshed, but Jack still milked his 80-odd Jersey cows in a walk-through cowshed.

Jack's shed was a real relic, a thing of the past, constructed from the same off-cuts that were leaning against the house. The idea of a walk-through shed is that the cow enters a booth where one hind leg is tied back against one of the partitioning rails. Once the milking is over the cow is released through a door in the front of the booth. Once she would have been hand-milked, but even Jack had advanced to a fairly primitive milking machine.

The purpose of my visit was to dehorn two of his Jersey heifers, a routine procedure on a dairy farm. The cow's head is held with a gadget called a nose-grip, which is like a pair of pliers with knobs on the end of the jaws which fit into the nostrils of the cow. A rope goes through holes in the handles, so that pulling on the rope holds the nose-grip shut. The end of the rope is usually tied to a beam above the cow's head.

A cow's horns have nerves running up from the skin in a groove of bone. It is relatively easy to feel this groove and inject local anaesthetic around the nerve so the horn can be cut off without any pain to the cow, using an abrasive wire with a hand-grip on each end.

Jack had constructed a pen on the side of the cowshed from his inexhaustible supply of slab timber, especially for my visit. Thinking the heifers would be nervous on their own, he had included three adults. As soon as we moved into the yard one of these cows reared on her hind legs and managed to get her front legs over the top rail. This was too much for Jack's elderly timber. One by one the rails broke or the nails pulled out. When there was no further resistance, the cow calmly stepped over the bottom rail and led her little troupe to freedom.

Jack was furious. 'Look what the silly bitch has done now,' he said in his squeaky little voice. This was more than I could cope with and I began to giggle helplessly.

'This is no laughing matter,' he said sharply, his voice rising half an octave. Fiddling with my fly in the hope he might think I needed a piddle, I escaped to the back of the cowshed and leant helplessly against the wall.

By the time I had recovered, the little heading dog had turned the mob and was bringing them back. 'Forget the cows, Jack. Let's just run each heifer into a milking bale.'

In the end the heifers were more placid without the adults and so long as Jack remained silent I was able to control myself. Clouds of borer dust filled the air, highlighting the beams of sunlight coming through the holes in the iron roof, as I attached the rope from the nose-grip to the beam above the front of the cow bale. Once the horn was anaesthetised it was a simple, if strenuous, job to throw the loop of abrasive wire over it then furiously cut through, hoping to stay as near to the horn/skin margin as possible. The first three horns went without any problem at all, but I must have missed the nerve on the fourth one because I was only part-way through the horn when the little heifer bellowed and threw her head in the air before driving it sharply down toward the ground.

At that point the entire cowshed collapsed around us. As I dragged myself out from under the rubble of borer-ridden timber, I was amazed to hear shrill laughter emerging from beneath a heap of iron. Jack struggled out and stood up, tears tracking through the borer dust covering his face. His gaunt, stooped frame shook as a child giggled uncontrollably inside him.

'You know,' he said, 'I've been seriously thinking of taking up beef farming.'

Aubrey Blythe was as different from Jack Delaney as it was possible to be. He had a very large body with a matching voice. The men of

South Westland often spoke to each other over long distances and the arrival of the telephone did little to change the habit. Aubrey was aware that his voice booming from the handpiece was unmistakable, so he would launch straight into a conversation without identifying himself.

'I want you to come down and have a look at my bull. Bring that new testing gadget. Come after dark. I don't want the neighbours to see you arrive. Can't say any more. Party line you know.' He hung up. Brevity was not one of Aubrey's attributes so I assumed he was concerned that someone might be listening in.

Unlike Jack, Aubrey was already a successful beef breeder, well known for his Angus cattle. He had proudly shown me Hercules, his new bull, on my last visit. The clue in his cryptic phone message was the reference to the 'testing gadget'. It could only mean that he was concerned about the fertility of Hercules.

The clinic had recently purchased an electro-ejaculator, an instrument used in the collection of semen from bulls. It was a large stainless steel probe on the end of a long cable, at the other end of which was a console with knobs that you could turn to vary the strength and frequency of an electrical current flowing into the probe. Once inserted into the rectum of a suitably restrained bull, the probe lay in close contact with a group of nerves on the floor of the pelvis. These were the nerves that controlled ejaculation.

In South Westland it seems that any question of the fertility of a man's bull reflects badly on himself, almost to the point where it throws his own fertility into question, so I arrived there after dark, swung around the back of the house and pulled up in the carpark. Before I turned them off the headlights shone through the drizzle, resting briefly on Aubrey pacing about in his raincoat.

'Did anyone see you come in?'

'No, the road was empty when I arrived.'

'Good,' he said. 'Right. Come with me.'

He led the way on his tractor to the cattle crush. Munching quietly on a slab of hay in the yard leading up to the crush was Hercules.

'We've nearly finished the season and I haven't had a single calf from his girls yet. I've had to shift the whole herd away from the road in case someone works out what's happening.'

'Did you see him working?' I asked.

'Cripes yes,' he replied, involuntarily moving his pelvis in imitation. 'I spent the whole autumn watching him through the binoculars.'

This confession suddenly seemed to embarrass him.

'Well, let's have a look at him then,' I said hastily, as a diversion.

Aubrey always had the best of everything, and this was a beautiful cattle crush made out of iron pipes with sheet metal sidings that opened in various areas to provide access for the animals. Hercules lumbered amiably up the race and allowed himself to be trapped in the head bale.

Aubrey backed the tractor up and shone the light mounted on its back mudguard down onto the midsection of the crush.

I lubricated the probe, the stainless steel glinting in the tractor light, and inserted it into Hercules, who grunted slightly. I attached the wires with their two crocodile clips to the tractor battery, climbed into the seat and placed the now buzzing console on my knee. I leant forward and flicked the switch. Nothing happened. Then slowly, step by step, I increased the power. A wave of contractions rippled up his massive, black back and steam began to rise through the drizzle. At the end of each wave Hercules emitted a surprisingly human groan.

I looked down. Aubrey was crouched in the patch of light, his arm holding the test tube and funnel moving in unison with Hercules'

lunging penis. As the surges of power heightened, the bull's move-
ments became more urgent and dramatic. The drizzle became hard,
drumming rain, running in streams from Hercules' heaving, slick,
glossy back. There was a flash of lightning behind us, followed by a
kettledrum roll of thunder. I felt like the conductor of an orchestra.

Suddenly Hercules gave vent to a prolonged, primitive roar and
ejaculated. Aubrey looked up at me. In the odd yellowish light he
looked drained and exhausted. But there was more. There was a
furtiveness enhanced by the black socket that was his eye, by the
craggy curve of his nose with the shadow thrown onto it by the mole
on his cheek.

In a hoarse whisper he said, 'You don't think the cops'll come and
catch us playing around with animals, do you?'

Coming from the city as I did, the attractions – and skills – of horse-
riding have always escaped me. Many farms on the West Coast needed
horses. They were the staple stockman's method of transport as the
country was often too boggy, hilly or threaded by rivers for motor-
bikes or four-wheel drives to be of any use.

The O'Malley brothers had a run-off behind Ross up the Mikinui
River and I drove down there to vaccinate the calves against brucel-
losis. Reaching this run-off took care of the whole exhaust system on
my beautiful Peugeot, so I was not in the happiest frame of mind
when we pulled up on the banks of the Mikinui, which was milky
grey-green and in full flood, rumbling with the boulders moving
along the bottom. Three horses were tethered to the super bin.

'We've given you the quiet one,' said the elder brother.

'Are we seriously going to cross that river?' I asked.

'Oh, we do it all the time,' they said. 'These horses know all about
it. Just sit on her and you'll make it.'

So I loaded my pack on my back with the vaccination gear in it, sat obediently on the horse assigned to me, and told Kelly to stay by the car. Little Kelly sat there in the drizzle, shaking a bit, as we left. The horse did exactly as they said. It swam the river while I sat on it trying to imagine that it was an armchair, not a horse. It pulled itself up on the other bank and shook as though this were a totally routine thing to do.

The elder brother said, 'We've got to muster the cows now.'

'Well,' I thought, 'I'm glad I put aside the whole day for this.'

'Stand here,' he instructed, indicating a spot in the paddock, 'and when the mob comes, divert them into the yard.'

I sat on the horse and felt the cold drizzle seeping into my bones. The brothers rode away over the horizon until, about half an hour later, there was a dull, thundering noise in the distance and a mob of about 200 Hereford cattle appeared. They got bigger and bigger as they came closer and closer, then smaller and smaller as they disappeared past me towards the other horizon.

Any yelling and shouting that I'd done had been of no avail – it was probably drowned by the hammering of their hooves on the ground. As I stood there wondering what to do, a flattened heap of tussock in front of me moved, and out from underneath it came Kelly. Somehow she had swum the river, had been washed about two miles downstream, and then worked her way back up to me through the tussock.

Without much help from me, the cattle were finally yarded. Then came the time to separate the calves from their mothers. This was the first demonstration I had seen of a cutting horse in action and I soon realised their importance to beef farmers.

Terry O'Malley positioned himself on his horse, guarding the open gateway leading into the next pen. Without any apparent direction from the rider, the horse moved away from the gate and a cow from the mob would seize her opportunity and make a break through the gap. Before her calf could follow the pony moved forward and blocked its escape. This sequence was repeated time after time until there were only calves left in the yard.

As the calves were pushed up the race, I gave each an injection as it moved through. Terry followed behind, pouring a teacup of a yellowish fluid over each calf.

'Hey, isn't that one of those new pour-on lice treatments?' I asked.

'Yeah, makes life easy, doesn't it?' he replied.

'It says on the side of the can that you've got to wear rubber gloves and a mask or you can get really crook.'

'Cripes, is that a fact? What are the signs?'

'Well, you feel like throwing up and your eyes go all blurry.'

'Jeez, I'm feeling like that already. I thought it was just me hangover.'

After the calves were finished, we castrated five yearling bulls and packed up to leave. I was worried about Kelly.

'I don't think my little dog'll be able to swim back again.'

'Don't worry. We'll pass her up to you on the horse.'

But this stoical animal that would happily handle flooded rivers and heaving, throbbing cattle was terrified of Kelly on the saddle, and it was only one of the better horsemen who succeeded in taking Kelly on his saddle and crossing the river safely again.

The furthest south the practice went was Paringa, below Fox Glacier and almost to the Haast, where there was a single large farm. If a farmer was a member of the vet club, his subscription took care of the mileage, but because visits to Paringa were so infrequent the Ryder brothers hadn't paid their subscription. But they rang up one day to say they had a cow with a prolapsed uterus and would the vet come down.

A prolapsed uterus presents quite a challenge to a vet. When it's turned inside out and hangs down behind the legs, a cow's uterus is an enormous structure, and to reproduce, which is all that beef cows do, the cow needs a very good working uterus. So the Ryders were prepared to pay the $100 or so of mileage in the hope that the vet would return the uterus to full working order.

Once again when I arrived a horse was produced for me. 'D'you think you can use that flash new drug that Vince had – what was its name?' James asked.

'Rompun,' I replied.

'Yep, you're on the case. One jab and the cow will just lie down and go to sleep. All you have to do is just ride up to her and lean over and give the injection.'

'Okay,' I said, and we mounted our steeds, me with my syringe loaded, and galloped off over the horizon.

Well, galloping was not a technique I had mastered, so when the horse broke into a bumpy stride I bounced around on top hanging on for grim death. The other horsemen, who were about a hundred yards ahead of me, galloped in a very smooth, flowing motion. When we arrived at our destination like a posse out of the Wild West the leader of the team held a hand up exactly like the American cavalry, and everyone reined in behind him. Fortunately my horse was of a sociable disposition and stopped of its own volition.

'See that clump of cabbage trees?' the boss said. 'The cow's lying down behind that. Just work your horse up close. She won't worry about the horse, so you can just lean down and give her an injection.'

After 20 minutes or so of kicking and thumping I persuaded the horse to strike out on its own and walk towards the clump of cabbage trees. I felt I was being tested a bit, judging by the giggles and smiles behind hands over mouths.

Finally I found myself beside the cow, who appeared to be totally relaxed about a horse being close by. To cover another six feet and get really close to her took another 20 minutes of kicking and cajoling and whispering, but finally I found myself looking down at this large, red body. I leaned over as far as I could and, full of confidence, raised my arm to shove the injection into her rump when suddenly the stirrup gave way and I landed right on top of her.

I jabbed at her furiously, but only managed to bend the needle over. The cow then rose majestically to her feet with me on top of her. The assembled audience yodelled and hooted and hollered.

'Stay on, Davey! Ride her back to the yards!'

I declined graciously and equally graciously slipped to the ground. The poor cow had to walk three or four miles back to the yards with a huge oozing bag of a uterus banging against her hocks. Once there we pushed her up the race, gave her the injection and she lay down very nicely, in sharp contrast to my first expedition to South Westland.

Returning the uterus to its usual position involves putting on a big apron, kneeling behind the cow, bundling the whole uterus into the apron and, after carefully washing and disinfecting it, pushing it inch by inch back through the vulva, compressing it as you go to get rid of the accumulated fluid.

After about an hour and a half the uterus was safely back inside. Some of the placental attachment points had been lost in the process, but luckily there had been no rips in the uterus itself.

The real joy came a year later, when I met James at the Hokitika races.

'How did that cow do – the one with the womb out?' I asked.

'Had a calf at foot when I last saw her and no sign of a prolapse.

But,' he added with a suggestion of a wink, 'she seemed a bit nervous of the horse, so I couldn't get too close.'

I suspect that there is an as yet undiscovered law of veterinary medicine that controls the ratio of success to failure. It probably varies between vets, but I am certain that no vet exists who's had 100 per cent success. I would like to call it Marshall's Law of Humiliation, and would define it thus: as the number of successful outcomes increases, so too does the risk of cataclysmic failure. Marshall's Law of Humiliation was proved one afternoon by Vince and a budgie.

'Here, have a look at this, will you?' Vince said, carrying a bird cage from the hospital room. 'You're always telling me you'd rather look at small animals. Is this small enough?'

The budgie inside would have been called Elephant Man if it were human. A large warty growth sprouted from just above its beak.

'What did you tell the owner we were going to do?'

'I didn't tell her we were going to do anything. But I did tell her you were very good with small animals and would be doing the job. I'm pregnancy-testing cows all day, so I'll see you tonight.'

I had never had to anaesthetise a bird before, so I started looking up the books. I am sure that published somewhere is a comprehensive account of the subject, but it was not in the Hokitika veterinary library. All I could find in an elderly veterinary dictionary was a reference to using ether.

I went looking for Fred, the receptionist, storeman and theatre nurse. He was in the staff room, drinking medicine out of a spoon.

'I had to go to the doctor this morning. I've felt terrible ever since you gave me that white muck that time I had a hangover.'

'You didn't tell the doctor I gave it to you, did you? They don't like vets treating humans.'

'Well, I did, actually.'

I picked up the bottle. It was exactly the same as my original medicine.

'This should make you feel better. Actually, I was looking for you to give me a hand with this budgie. You haven't seen any ether, have you?'

Fred came back holding a brown bottle. I found a pillbox in the cupboard, placed a wad of cottonwool in the bottom and soaked it in ether. Holding the bird firmly in one hand, I pushed its head into the pillbox.

'This is how the book said to do it.'

Fred looked sceptical. 'How do you know when it's ready?'

'I don't know. When it stops wriggling, I suppose. Can you get the electric scalpel connected up?'

Fred plugged the power in and laid the black plastic control box on the table beside the now unconscious bird. He positioned the foot switch near my foot and handed me the electrode that would produce the sparks to burn the lump off.

'Hurry up, the anaesthetic won't last very long.'

I leaned forward and flicked the switch.

There was a muffled boom and a shower of feathers shot across the room. When I looked back the bird had entirely disappeared.

'Jesus,' said Fred, reverently.

I had a fleeting image of Mum's face, as she looked for her rubbish tin.

'Do you think Vince would have warned her that there was a bit of a risk with the anaesthetic?'

I would probably have been content to have lived my entire veterinary life in Hokitika. I enjoyed the social life, which was always interesting and often hilarious. I enjoyed the relaxed approach to life of West Coast farmers; indeed West Coasters in general. I remember turning up three times to a farmer to vaccinate his cows for lepto, because the first two times I forgot to bring the vaccine. This meant that he had his entire herd in the yards all ready – his routine for the day had been completely altered to accommodate me – and I'd turned up without the vaccines. Not once, but twice. Each time he just said, 'Never mind. Come and have a cup of tea. Don't worry about it.'

When Roy Bailey and his wife Jan offered me a job helping them back at their practice in Christchurch it took me a while before I finally accepted and it was with mixed feelings that I packed up my gear, took the radio telephone out of the car and drove over the pass to Christchurch.

I felt especially sad about leaving Vince, who was not only my financial saviour but also my philosophical mentor. We had worked very well together, but ultimately I wouldn't miss the constant limitations imposed by the need for dairy farmers to make an income, the constant battle of making do and half-treating and half-diagnosing because there wasn't the money to do a proper job – in short, the frustrations of a large animal practice.

That was the appeal of small animals. They weren't restricted in value to what you could get for them at the freezing works. Their true value lay in what their owners thought of them in emotional terms. In my small animal practice I often say, 'This is a time when you have to calculate your love in dollars.' And of course as the years have gone by the dollar price has risen dramatically. But from a vet's point of view treating small animals is a very satisfying branch of veterinary medicine.

And at the end of the day I suppose I was really going back home – back to my childhood, back to Linwood.

7

Small is Better

The Worcester Street clinic in 1972 was radically different from the place I remembered as a student, mostly because it had become very busy. I had to adjust overnight from a country practice with an average of 10 calls a day, with a half-hour drive between each, to 50 consultations a day with no time at all between them. If I extended the consult time longer than ten minutes, Roy would rap on the glass doors of the instrument panel separating our two rooms.

So we had to move really fast. The evening clinic opened at 4pm and went through till 7pm. People would immediately start pouring in – first come, first served: we didn't have an appointment system in those days – and by 5 o'clock the waiting room would be full with standing room only. Soon afterwards the stairs that led up to my flat over the clinic would have three people on every step and the carpark would be full, not of cars but of people. People would be lined up shoulder-to-shoulder along the fence that separated us from the neighbour, on a wet night or a fine night.

The nurse behind the counter did a wonderful job – unbelievable. We had no till, so the money was thrown into a butter box beneath the counter. By the end of the night it overflowed with notes.

It was a matter of learn fast or get out, and looking back it was a superb learning experience. I saw so much of every possible small animal disease that provided I recognised the symptoms I had no alternative but to learn. I became very experienced at routines such as listening to chests or palpating abdomens.

Just as quickly I was forced to come to terms with dealing with the wide range of people who brought their beloved animals in to us: I discovered that oddball characters were not confined to the West Coast.

Pets are a great source of comfort for people who live alone. Some are lonely because they have outlived their friends; others have personalities that do not attract friends. For many a pet is more important than a human. Dogs and cats do not make judgments. I quickly learned not to be critical myself. Even the reclusive and the alienated will come out of hiding when concerned for their pet. Drunk or sober, mad or sane, shrivelled with grief or entirely normal, pets make lovers of us all.

Old Mr Carpenter was an Old Contemptible. At least, that is what the badge on his lapel said. I had to ask him what it meant, and he told me about his time in World War I, when he was a member of a cavalry unit fighting Kaiser Bill. Apparently the phrase came from the Kaiser saying that they were a contemptible little army.

Mr Carpenter adored animals. He told me that during World War I the horses all developed strangles, so he spent his whole day wiping their noses. In more recent times the size of his charges had changed but the disease turned out to be similar. He now tended to the health of a large flock of feral cats, which he would bring in for treatment when they were sick enough to be caught. For the rest, he spent his entire time 'wiping their little noses'.

The old man would arrive in his Austin 1100 with his overcoat and scarf on, his shoes all polished, hair neatly done, moustache waxed, and we would talk about the problems of the respiratory diseases in his cats, which were never going to get better. I asked him how many cats he had, and he thought roughly 75.

I did a house call for him once. He lived at the top of Mt Pleasant Road, which I took to be quite a good address. When I arrived I parked beneath a group of huge old pine trees and walked down a path that was not very well laid out, to say the least. The path led me to what I thought was a shed, and as I went around the corner a tidal wave of cats poured out of the doors and the windows, fleeing terrified into the surrounding bush and scrub.

When I poked my head through the window Mr Carpenter was ill in bed. He was actually lying in a heap of sacks in the corner. Two cats remained in the room. One, the reason I was summoned, was moribund and died while I was there, and the other wasn't much better. Mr Carpenter lived in absolute squalor. There was no glass in the windows. There was no heating. He had shovelled about a cubic metre of dirt into the corner of the room, and this was the cats' dirt box. When it became thoroughly soiled, he would shovel it out and replace it with another pile – something he seemed to have forgotten to do recently.

While I was there the Nurse Maude lady arrived with some lunch. This regular visit was probably the only thing that kept him alive, as he told me that he was content to have no more than a brandy and a cigar for breakfast.

Finally, Mr Carpenter was prevailed upon to go into an old people's home. The neighbours promised to feed his cats for him, and they stuck to this in the main, although some of the truly wild cats were shot. Others were successfully domesticated.

Some years later I met Mr Carpenter in the Square. He was sitting on a bench with the same overcoat and scarf, with his hair neatly done. He looked fatter, but sadder. He asked me if I would take him up to his old place. When we arrived his little hut was gone, the trees were gone. A developer had bought the land and bulldozers were carving it up. Of his cats there was no sign.

I hadn't long been at Worcester Street when Sydney Winterburn arrived about 10 o'clock one night, unannounced. It was a really miserable night with strong winds and heavy rain. When I let him in, and took his soaking coat and scarf off him, Sydney told me he had walked from Saxon Street, about four or five blocks away, because his little cat was sick. He had the cat in a haversack on his back. I placed the cat on the table and examined it. It was having a lot of trouble breathing and was almost unconscious.

By the look of his frayed cuffs, Sydney didn't have any money for a range of expensive tests, so I took a chance and put a needle between the cat's ribs into its chest and pulled back on the plunger. The syringe filled with pale pink watery pus.

'Mr Winterburn,' I intoned, with all the solemnity I could find, 'this is a very bad sign. Your cat has effusive pleurisy, which is always fatal.'

Nowadays, we know there are several causes for the presence of this type of fluid some of them very treatable, but at that time it was assumed to show an incurable infection.

The news did not seem to shock him as much as I had expected. He gave me the impression that he had become accustomed to losing things that were precious to him. After we put the cat down I invited him upstairs to have a cup of tea and to dry out before going home. He spent some time studying my old textbooks.

Sydney told me that he was a herpetologist, which luckily I knew to be a snake enthusiast – an odd enthusiasm, I thought, for someone in New Zealand to have. But he was very keen on snakes and borrowed several books to take home, as the haversack was now empty. I had the impression that he was a remittance man – that he was being paid a stipend to stay away from home in England. He suggested that his parents were very well-to-do military types in the old country, but by this time Sydney wasn't young anyway, so maybe they'd already died. He struck me as a real character.

His cheques were a work of art. He had at least four different rubber stamps – his name and address, his 'not negotiable', 'account payee only' and the date were all separately stamped on.

Sydney also had a dog, a little fox terrier, which was his constant companion. He rang up one day. 'Couldn't bring my dog in, could I? I don't want to take your time up unnecessarily, Doctor, but I fear he's not very well.'

'What do you think is wrong with him Sydney?' I asked.

'Well, that's just it. I can't see anything wrong. He doesn't seem ill at all, but he's just lying very quietly under the bed.'

Sydney's dog had a ruptured spleen and was bleeding internally and without his high index of suspicion it would have died. It was from experiences such as this that I learnt how important it was not to underrate owners' suspicions. If they think the dog is not well, it is not well, and woe betide any vet who neglects to take full cognisance of their opinion.

Sydney would walk his dog late in the evening and often call in for a cup of tea after clinic, when I was on my own. I happened to mention to the police dog handlers who also occasionally called in on their evening rounds that Sydney had been in.

'Oh, we know Sydney quite well. He's something of a peeping

Tom, and he uses his little dog as an alibi. If anyone catches him lurking around the window he just says that he had to follow his dog in because it chased a hedgehog and he's very sorry, and off he goes. But he's been caught in compromising situations maybe four or five times now.'

Sydney came in to me one day looking very spruce and well dressed. He said he was to appear in court later that day as a character witness for a friend who'd been accused of interfering with small boys. Sydney was adamant that this was a trumped-up charge.

'How do you know that, Sydney?'

Sydney suddenly become an amateur Perry Mason. It would be physically impossible for this man to do what was described in the charge, he said, because he was afflicted with a huge scrotal hernia that caused him so much pain that any attempt at intercourse would be excruciating for him. It occurred to me that this was an odd piece of information for Sydney to possess about his friend.

Like many of my old clients, Sydney finally stopped coming, and despite all his vagaries and probable nastinesses, I missed him. I suppose either he died or the police finally caught up with him.

Living upstairs above the clinic at Worcester Street made me a natural target for all the after-hours emergency calls. When I lived on my own this was no great problem, in fact it was quite often a diversion. I was sitting upstairs one night when I happened to notice a middle-aged woman wandering about in the middle of the road in front of the clinic. I went down and spoke to her.

I was startled by her response. 'Oh, I'm just waiting for the doctor to arrive to put my husband down.' She seemed to be quite distraught – understandable under the circumstances – so I invited her back to the clinic and we sat downstairs in the waiting room until the doctor arrived. As we sat on one of the forms, looking out the window, I chatted away to her to make her comfortable. Some time had elapsed and the doctor had still not appeared, so I said, 'How long ago did you ring him?'

'I haven't phoned him, I've just talked to him.'

'How you mean? By telepathy?'

'Yes,' she said.

About this stage I began to feel a bit annoyed. 'Well, let's go over and see how your husband is.'

We started to cross the road when suddenly she ran off and hailed a passing taxi.

'Help!' she shouted to the driver. 'This bloke's been trying to molest me. He's also offered me drugs!'

Feeling disgusted with the whole business, I left her and walked off. The taxi driver also left quickly.

The woman continued wandering up and down the road, yelling and ranting, so I decided that I couldn't just leave her there. I rang the Samaritans who, although obviously only a telephone service, tried to be very helpful, suggesting I bring her back inside. That was the last thing I was going to do, so finally I phoned the police and asked them to contact the dog handler on duty and have him call past.

Paul Kane, the dog handler, was quite superb. I don't know whether it was the uniform or what, but when he spoke to her she became obedient and civil. They entered her house and soon afterwards he returned to his vehicle. I waved him over and asked him what had happened.

'Apparently every time there's a full moon the woman goes a bit crazy and so the husband locks her in the house. Tonight she found the key and got out after he'd gone to sleep.'

Paul had woken the husband, who then put his wife to bed, after which everything had settled down. The only sadness was that my little Abyssinian cat, who had only ever lived above the clinic, followed me out onto the road that night. The next day she ventured out again on her own and was run over and killed.

I really enjoyed dealing with police dogs and their handlers. The handlers sometimes lived dangerously when they found themselves holding on to the lead of a dog pulling them towards someone in hiding who could possibly be aiming a gun at them, but they were a very casual and blasé group of men, whose company I enjoyed socially as well as professionally.

Dale Pohio, one of my police friends, became a dog handler about the same time I started at Worcester Street. His first dog, Duke, was an awesome beast. He had been a gift dog, which meant that at the age of eighteen months or so he had been given to the police, probably because he had become too aggressive for his owners.

When Dale travelled up to Trentham to pick Duke up they said to him, 'There's your dog in a cage. Go and get it.' And the dog was *vicious*. He ripped Dale's trousers, tore the front out of his tunic, and left him cut and scratched and bleeding. But finally Dale got a lead on to him, and eventually Duke turned out to be one of the best police dogs in New Zealand, although he remained somewhat unpredictable throughout his life. On one occasion the dog was taken along to an illegal assembly – the statute of the Crimes Bill they used when trying to deal with large groups of bikies. Duke had a ball. He bit a number of bikies and four policemen as well.

Whenever Duke was brought in I used to jump up on the bench in the consulting room because he usually tried to have a go at my legs. 'Well, what's wrong with the dog today?' I would ask, sitting up there like a Buddha. If we ever had to examine the dog thoroughly we'd need three handlers to grab hold of him.

But finally Dale and the dog, and even the dog and I, reached a good understanding. In the end he was used as a stud dog at Trentham, where he produced a successful line of dogs for the police.

The relationship between a dog handler and his dog is very special. They have to spend 12 to 15 weeks together on a special training course at Trentham, which means that the dog handlers spend all this time away from their families and homes. This results in a lot of emotional involvement with the dog. For a number of handlers, losing their dog often means that they decide to go to another section of the police rather than try to forge a new relationship with another dog. So if the dog becomes sick, what the vet does could become crucially important.

Major came in one day with his handler, apparently constipated. He strained all the time, had difficulty urinating and appeared distressed and uncomfortable. When I did a rectal examination I could feel a fluid swelling running up the side of the rectum between the pelvis and the rectal wall. This usually meant a perineal hernia – the lining between the abdomen and the pelvic space had weakened, with the result that the bladder had turned over and been pushed back into the area beside the rectum.

We filled the bladder with air and took an X-ray, only to discover that the bladder was in its normal position. So apart from the bladder we had another fluid-filled organ beside the rectum. An exploratory operation allowed us to drain a small amount of fluid from the centre of this organ and to collect a sample – a piece of the wall of the organ – before closing the dog up again.

At this stage we thought that the problem was probably caused by a cancer, and more or less implied this to the handler, who was understandably upset. But when we sent the specimen to the lab they reported back that it wasn't a tumour – in fact they didn't know what it was. So we started hunting through the books and finally came up with the answer – it was a prostatic cyst. The prostate of a dog sits just behind the bladder and it's possible for pockets of a considerable size to form in the tissue. What fooled us was that these football-sized, fluid-filled pockets nearly always go forwards so they're felt lying up beside the bladder or even further up towards the kidney, whereas in this case it went backwards, pushing the skin out beside the anus.

Once we had the diagnosis, the treatment was simple. We made a hole so that the fluid in the bag could continue to drain out, and at the same time castrated the dog. Castration removes the prostate – well, it shrinks the prostate almost to nil. Major was fixed, and the handler went back to work overjoyed that he still had his good dog and didn't have to go to Trentham again.

One of Keith Nicholl's early dogs developed an enlarged prostate and had to be castrated. I've always been impressed that after we took the stitches out, this dog went out on the same night and caught 17 bad guys. Obviously training is more important than testosterone when it comes to police dogs!

I think the worst emotional moment for me, among several emotional moments, was when I attended the funeral of a dog handler who had died. As the coffin left the chapel it passed out between rows of dog handlers and their dogs dressed in their dress uniform – a cover trimmed in the police colours. The sergeant had his own dog, but he also had Mark's dog standing in front of him. Seeing the dog without its handler was a sharp, painful moment for me.

I had been at Worcester Street about six months when Faye reappeared from my past. We had met at the Domain Terrace dance where Ray Columbus began his career and had gone out together for about a year. Between sightings she had been teaching on high-country farms, travelled to Australia, married a painter, lived on fire towers on the Great Divide in Victoria and on lighthouses in Bass Strait. Arna was born during the fire-watching period.

Fayee's life had been the complete antithesis of mine – perhaps that was what intrigued me – but we thoroughly enjoyed each other's company. Arna, who was six at the time, selected me as her next father during a holiday on the West Coast where we rented a cottage overlooking the sea, twelve miles north of Greymouth. The roof leaked into buckets and pots placed all over the floor. There was even one on the end of the bed. The wallpaper rolled off the walls, except where it was held up with drawing pins. Faye played Cat Stevens and Janis Joplin and Arna watched us both with increasing curiosity.

Despite the weather and the music we had a great time. I enjoyed being shown a relaxed, pleasuring way of life so different from my pressured, intense existence in which, living above the clinic, I was never off duty, even at night.

I remember the first night Faye stayed overnight with me at Worcester Street. When she looked in the fridge to organise some breakfast, all she found was three bags of dogs' blood that were stored there ready for transfusing.

'What would you like for breakfast?' she asked me. 'Blood on toast?'

Roy and Jan had lived above the clinic when they first arrived in Christchurch. It was a very cosy, comfortable little flat – two bedrooms, a lounge and a bathroom that Faye and I later painted purple. The lounge had an old-fashioned gas fire, and I loved the nights when I could look out of the window and see the street lights glowing weakly in the Christchurch fog. The combination of the foggy night and the little gas fire brought to mind Sherlock Holmes in Baker Street.

When Arna and Faye moved in my standard of living improved considerably. However, Arna found life living above a veterinary clinic a bit disconcerting. She was quite fussy with food and I remember going out to the carpark one night to help someone put their dog into the car. When I looked up the light shining down on the carpark seemed to be a bit obscured. Later, when I checked, I found it was covered in lettuce leaves and the unwanted remains of Arna's meals, which she had surreptitiously thrown out the window. Her other habit that proved a problem was that she would stand in the shower with her foot on the plughole. Eventually the water would overflow, but because we were upstairs it flowed down into the waiting room below.

Faye had a friend, David, who was the head chef at Noah's Hotel and when they were invited to tea she was quite concerned to present the food well. We had a little low table that we knelt around, and a little fluffy cat of Arna's called Cassie. The steaks were beautifully cooked and placed on the table. We knelt on our cushions and lifted our forks ready to eat. Just at that moment a furry paw sneaked over the edge of David's plate, two claws dug into the steak and the cat raced off, carrying the steak.

David said he didn't mind that the cat had stolen his steak so much, but he was a bit disconcerted at the way Faye had climbed out the window onto the roof trying to get the food back again.

Murray Pringle and his wife Barbara, both vets, had come back to Roy's practice after doing post-graduate training at Melbourne vet school. Murray trained in surgery and Barbara in medicine. They showed Roy and me a new face of veterinary practice – a scientific, logical approach. It was not long before they were made partners and Bailey, Marshall & Pringle was born, a partnership that lasted 15 years.

Jean Smith and her dog Jonjon were inseparable friends. She lived on her own in Sumner, so the dog played a very important part in her life. She came to see me one day and said, 'You might think this is silly, but when I've got him cuddled up on my lap, I can feel his heart banging away on his right side. There's no beating on the left side at all.'

'Well, it might be nothing at all,' I said, 'but it might be a good idea to do an X-ray. At worst there might be something between his heart and his ribs on the left-hand side.'

'What do you mean "something"?' she asked.

'Well, anything's possible, I suppose.' The word 'tumour' hovered, unspoken, between us. 'Let's do the X-ray first.'

Jonjon was a nice, obliging, little pekinese who lay down for us so I could take an X-ray. This was in the early days of Worcester Street, when the machine took about three seconds to produce a sufficient number of rays to penetrate the dog. The exposed films were then developed in white plastic trays that were filled with fresh chemical each time. It was all very uncertain: the temperature was very approximate, the developing was poor, to say the least, and the actual technique of taking the X-ray wasn't much better. But it was better than nothing – many other clinics of a similar size had no X-ray facilities at all.

On Jonjon's film we saw a vague white sphere, which was the heart, in the middle of a black triangle, which was the lung. It seemed to be a very big heart, but I was uncertain about this so I took the X-ray to Princess Margaret Hospital. I must admit I was so naive that I didn't even appreciate the extraordinarily poor quality of my X-ray, but the superintendent, Heath Thompson, was very kind.

'Well,' he said. 'it looks to us as if the dog has a cardiomyopathy.'

'What's that?' I asked.

'An enlarged heart.'

'Oh, okay.'

So I went home again, but I was puzzled and discussed the film again with Roy. 'The dog still has good energy levels. It's not tired or flat. It doesn't cough, It hasn't got any fluid in its abdomen, and it hasn't got any of the other signs that you normally associate with heart failure.'

'I can see these dark pieces in the middle of the white of the heart,' said Roy. 'It must be gas. Maybe it's the oesophagus caught up somewhere.'

I gave the dog some barium, which would show up on an X-ray, but the barium went straight through, without sticking, so I was still in the dark about the position of the oesophagus. An hour later I took another X-ray, thinking a different angle might show more.

When the film came out of the darkroom I was amazed at what I saw. There was a tortuous white band running right through the heart shadow, which must have been my barium which had advanced as far as the intestines. The gas we had seen was within the intestines, which in turn were within the pericardium, the bag that encloses the heart.

I looked up the books and discovered that this was a condition called pericardio-peritineo diaphragmatic hernia. Put simply, Jonjon had a hole in his diaphragm, the wall between his abdomen and his chest, but in line with this hole there was also a hole in the pericardium. He must have been born with this condition, and at some stage in his life the intestines must have made their way upward to lie around his heart.

So back I went to the hospital, where the experts were most impressed. This condition doesn't occur in humans so they were intrigued to see it in a dog. They were even more intrigued that our primitive X-ray system was able to show them a diagnosis they hadn't even suspected.

Heath Thompson, who was one of the top chest surgeons at the hospital, offered to operate on the dog, in what turned out to be simple surgery, albeit potentially nasty. It involved opening up the abdomen and bringing all the organs that were inside the bag surrounding the heart back into the abdomen, then gathering together the edges of the hole in the diaphragm and the pericardium and sewing them up as one unit. The big blood vessel leading from the liver the heart, the vena cava, which had gone through the hole, had to be carefully sewn round, but otherwise it was all relatively straightforward. But it was great to have an expert surgeon performing the operation.

Jonjon lived until he was 15 years old, a perfectly normal life span for a pekinese.

Things did not always go so well. Jean had another little dog called Marmite, a chihuahua cross. Marmite developed colitis, which is an inflammation of the bowel. He would pass mucus and pink blood on occasions and sometimes black tarry bowel motions. Poor Marmite found it uncomfortable to be hunched up, painfully straining away, so it was important to control the disease as soon as possible.

We first tried a drug called Salazapyrine, usually very good for bowel conditions, which worked well on Marmite, settling the inflammation down so the dog could live quite comfortably. But one of the unusual and, fortunately, infrequent side effects of Salazapyrine, along with other sulphur drugs, is that they reduce or eliminate tears from the eyes of the dog and, sadly, this is exactly what happened to Marmite. Withdrawing the drug does not reverse the condition.

The eventual consequence of a failure to produce tears is blindness. Most of the nutrition of the front of the eye comes from tears, and without them the corneas become scarred and damaged. So Marmite started to develop chronic pigmentation across the front of his eyes, which would inevitably make him go blind. The treatment at that time for this disease was to transplant the salivary duct – the tube taking saliva from the gland into the mouth – into the corner of the eye, so that every time the dog ate food, or thought about it, saliva would squeeze out into the corner of his eye. Surprisingly, saliva is little different from tears.

Murray performed a very time-consuming, laborious piece of surgery that ultimately proved very successful. But we were always gently reminded that we had caused the problem ourselves in the first place.

Murray performed a very time-consuming, laborious piece of surgery.

One of the first things I did when I moved to Christchurch was to persuade Roy to buy a brand-new ECG machine. This was a beautiful piece of equipment that worked very well and I became quite proficient at operating it. One day a woman brought in a 17-year-old dog that had been hit by a car. It lay on the floor of the cage, completely flat and lifeless. To begin with I thought it was just bruised and shaken up but when I put the ECG on it, I saw that something was dramatically wrong. Its heart was beating about 50 beats to the minute and each beat was a very odd shape. This meant that the accident had damaged the top part of the heart, and the odd-shaped, slow beat that I was seeing on the ECG was coming from a secondary pacing area in the bottom chambers.

A normal dog's heart beats between 80 and a 120 times a minute, so this dog was not pumping enough blood to make its body operate. Soon it would go into kidney failure and its brain wouldn't get enough oxygen or glucose, so something dramatic needed to be done if it was to live. The only treatment that was going to work, I decided, was a pacemaker.

The cardiology department at Christchurch Hospital had been very helpful in assessing ECGs for me from time to time so it was an obvious thing to ring the boss, Hamid Ikram.

'Can I have a pacemaker for a dog?'

'Well, we've probably got one or two lying around in the drawers here. Don't ask any questions about where they came from. We can't guarantee the battery life and you'll have to pay for the cable that joins the pacemaker to the heart, but our cardiologists are quite happy to put the pacemaker in for you if you think the dog will handle the anaesthetic.'

'Okay,' I said. 'That's great.'

So I warned the owner of the possible consequences, such as death, and set off to the hospital. Considering the dog was 17 the operation went surprisingly smoothly. The cable carrying the impulses was passed down the vena cava and the pacemaker itself was buried in the tissues under the skin of the neck. It took a bit of fiddling to make sure that the contact between the wire and the heart was as good as it could be, and soon the dog had a heart rate of about 110 to the minute. Better than that, the pacemaker was equipped with a radio receiver that would alter the rate and the strength of the beat depending on what was happening in the heart. It was a very sophisticated piece of equipment.

The dog was transformed. It had more energy than it had ever had before and, sadly, was run over three months later, chasing cats.

I had warned the owner that whatever happened to the dog, I wanted the pacemaker back, because I felt I could probably use it again some day. Unfortunately she brought the dog into the clinic in the weekend, and the nurses didn't know about the pacemaker, so sent the animal off to be disposed. Disposal in those days was via a by-products company that had an incinerator to turn organic by-products, such as offal, hooves and meat, into blood and bone. Pacemakers explode in heat, so we had to go straight around to the plant where, after sorting through all the bodies, we found our little dog and retrieved the pacemaker.

I was finishing an operation on a constipated dog one afternoon when Val, the head nurse, came rushing into the room. 'Quick, come out the front! We've got a big problem.'

A long, sleek greyhound lay on the table in front of its owner, Alex Walters. It was quite unconscious. I quickly examined it. It was breathing regularly with a normal heartbeat and there was no sign of any injury.

'What do you think happened?' I asked Alex.

'I don't know. I just fed my dogs this morning, and when I came back from work at lunchtime to have a look at them there she was, sound asleep.'

With nothing more to go on all we could do was treat the symptoms. With a drip of warm saline running into the vein in her front leg, we made her comfortable in a padded cage covered with blankets. I had more surgery to complete, so it was left to Val to keep an eye on her progress. Half an hour later Alex was back with two more dogs in exactly the same state, so at this stage it looked as if poisoning was involved. We didn't need a brick falling on our heads to work out that there was something seriously wrong.

I was sitting watching the sick dogs in their cages, each with a drip attached to its leg and swathed in blankets, when Val knelt beside me. She has been a nurse longer than I have been a vet, and there's not much that she hasn't seen.

Looking them over she said, 'You know, they look anaesthetised to me. See how their eyes are rolled down and their third eyelids are up? Look at their gums. They haven't lost any blood and they're not shocked. I think they're just anaesthetised.'

'You could be right,' I said. I remembered Vince telling me once that he had castrated some pigs and thrown the testicles over the fence. The farmer forgot to collect them up so his dogs ate them, after which they slept for two days. The trick to anaesthetising pigs was to put a huge dose of barbiturate straight into the testicle. As soon as they were asleep the testicle was whipped out, along with most of the drug, so they would wake up quite fast. Sleeping pills, Vince called them.

So I rang Alex at work and I said, 'What did you feed those dogs?'

'Oh,' he said, 'just horse meat from the usual guy we get it from.'

He gave me the name of the pet meat supplier, so I rang them up and said, 'That meat that you gave Mr Walters. Where did it come from?'

'It was a horse put down by a vet,' he said, 'but I bled it all out properly. It should have been okay.'

'What part of the animal did you give to Mr Walters?'

'The neck, actually.'

Everything was starting to come clear. The jugular vein in the neck is where the vet would typically give the injection to put the horse down. If some went outside the vein, it would remain in the meat in sufficiently high levels to produce what we'd seen here.

I was never able to track down the vet who gave the injection, but I am quite sure that a considerable part of that euthanasia injection ended up in the muscle tissue and was eaten by the dogs.

A day or two later they were fighting fit again.

Greyhound owners are always on the lookout for food for their dogs, which usually means unwanted cattle and horses. Jimmy McDonald had heard that a farmer who lived at the end of the peninsula at Godley Head had a cattle beast he didn't want. When Jimmy got there he found that the beast had actually fallen over a 60-foot bluff and had a fractured pelvis. It had been there for quite a while and was quite thin, so rather than butcher it immediately, Jimmy decided to take it to a friend's farm at Tuahiwi. They got a flat-decked trailer, loaded the steer on with some difficulty and set off.

Halfway through the Lyttelton tunnel the beast lunged over the side, succeeding in blocking the whole tunnel for an hour and a half while they reloaded it. They took it to Tuahiwi where they spent every day cutting grass and carrying it to the cattle beast. After about six weeks of this gentle treatment the animal died. It was still so thin that it was useless for meat. Jimmy told me the only time it ever moved was in the middle of the Lyttelton tunnel.

The Lyttelton tunnel featured in my life some time after this. The tunnel is a real bottleneck between Lyttelton and Christchurch, so when a horse float tipped over in it and trapped the horses there was a real panic. I arrived about 2 o'clock on a Saturday afternoon to find traffic banked up for about two miles out into the Heathcote Valley and about the full length of the wharf on the other side.

The axle of the horse float – a double horse float – had come loose from its attachment on one side, so with the axle now pointing out at 45 degrees the horse float steered in that direction and rolled over. There were two horses inside, lying one on top of the other. The fire brigade were already there with their hacksaws and jaws of life, but they wanted the horses sedated first.

This meant crawling in through the front window, which had popped out, in the half dark and placing an injection into the jugular veins of the two wild-eyed, panicking horses. I don't know how I ever did it, but we finally succeeded and put them half to sleep so that the firefighters could cut the horse float to pieces and get them out. One horse was completely untouched but the other one had a big wound on its shoulder that needed surgery.

My work often took me to Lyttelton, a fascinating little town with a strange mixture of people. A lot of seamen retire there. Jimmy McDonald was a Scot, whereas Willie Wilson said he came from the Shetland Islands. He'd been a whaler; he'd been to South Georgia Island, and he delighted in sitting down and telling me tales of his early whaling life. Willie lived on his own – his wife had died a few years earlier – and everything about him was immaculate. The house was white and painted, the paths were concrete and beautifully maintained, the garden was neat and there was never any rubbish.

Willie had a striking little dun pony. Every day he groomed it and polished its hooves with nugget. The bridle and tack were cleaned every day and its pen was scrubbed out – there was never any urine smell. Fresh hay was put down. Willie was obsessed with his dear little pony.

One day Jimmy, who had heard that Willie might be thinking of getting rid of his pony, climbed the steps to the crane where Willie worked on the wharves, stuck his head into Willie's cubicle and asked him if he had any horses. Willie said yes, he did, and was quite keen to talk about his beloved horse, until Jimmy said he'd like to buy it.

'What for?' Willie asked.

'To feed to the dogs, of course.'

He wasn't thrown off the crane, but neither man ever spoke to the other again.

8

The Longest House Call

Mr Marshall,' said Val, 'there's someone on the phone who wants you to do a house call to look at some dogs with arthritis.' I've never been very keen on house calls, so I was a bit grumpy when I got to the phone, but the someone turned out to be Colin Monteith from the Antarctic Division of the DSIR, who wondered whether I would be interested in going to the Antarctic to look after the health of the huskies they kept at Scott Base.

Some house call. I wasn't going to say no, but I had to explain to Faye that we weren't going to be having a Christmas holiday this year because I had this very serious work I had to do, which I wasn't going to be paid for. I omitted to mention that this event would occur every year, and so our holidays would be similarly limited for the foreseeable future.

After organising the necessary equipment and cold-weather clothing I found that I was exempted from going to Tekapo for the regular Antarctic training because I was only going to be there for a short time. At 5 o'clock one morning just before Christmas we boarded an American Starlifter – an enormous fat tadpole of an aeroplane with seating quite unlike any commercial plane I'd ever been on. This was a military transport aircraft, so the entire central area was filled with cargo, with the people strapped into webbing seats along the sides. There were only two windows in the body of the plane and the interior was lit by dim red lights.

Once the plane was airborne the noise was deafening so everyone was given earplugs – little wax things that you mould to fit your ears. So here we were, sitting in a huge uncomfortable plane that vibrated and shook and banged so loudly you couldn't have a conversation with your neighbour. Nor could you see out a window and the place was in half darkness, so it was about as boring as it can get – except that you had the expectation that you were going to arrive at this marvellous place at the other end. As we approached Antarctica we were told to put on our cold-weather gear, as they were going to drop the temperature in the plane to acclimatise us.

Finally the plane landed and we walked down the gangway to a dazzling, white vista – so white it hurt. To meet me – and this was a considerable honour – was the Scott Base dog team and the dog handler, John Stevens. John and I had spent some time together in Christchurch, because part of the agreement with the Antarctic Division was that I would teach the dog handler some simple veterinary skills such as whelping, the use of anaesthetics – local anaesthetics especially – suturing and antibiotic usage. So I arrived in state at Scott Base – sliding on the dog sledge across the sea ice.

In the early days – this was in 1972 – Scott Base was much more primitive than it is now. The living quarters consisted of a series of heated, insulated boxes connected by an uninsulated corrugated iron archway in which icicles hung from every nail head and knob. There were gutters along the side to carry the melted ice, and the archway was very cold. The kitchen, library, dining-room and bedroom cubicles, which all branched out from this central corridor, were lovely and warm and cosy – as was the general atmosphere of Scott Base. There was a wonderful enthusiasm among the volunteers here, in sharp contrast to the American base, which was made up mainly of military people, many of them naval conscripts with a very different attitude to their environment.

No vet had ever visited Scott Base before, but in anticipation that one would turn up eventually every dog that had died was buried and frozen for a post mortem. So one of my first jobs was to post-mortem about 20 frozen dogs. This proved difficult, first because it was almost impossible to cut into a frozen carcass, and secondly because the interval between a frozen dog and a rotten dog was quite short. So it wasn't long before I found myself spending a lot of time on my own at one end of the dining room. Showers were limited to one a week and as you had to shovel snow into a melter outside the building for about 30 minutes in order to enjoy seven minutes of shower, you really appreciated the luxury.

On my first trip to Scott Base there were enough dogs to run two separate sledge teams, each consisting of 11 dogs. It was high drama to go sledging at the end of the day's work. A towing rope would be laid out on the snow and attached to the front of the sledge and two large stakes driven into the snow both behind and in front of the sledge, with the lead dog's clip attached to the stake at the front.

The dogs were then brought up, harnessed in a soft, canvas-type material that formed a figure of eight around their front legs and under their chest, and then paired up the line with the lead dog, always a bitch, attached last. When there were visitors, and there often were – American rear admirals and other dignitaries always considered sledge-riding to be an important part of their Antarctic experience – they were given the job of holding on to the rope at the very front. This was a relatively unnecessary task, but it gave the dog handler the malicious pleasure of leading every male dog past the visiting dignitary and pausing to speak to him, thus allowing the dog to pee generously over the rear admiral's legs.

Once all the dogs, including the lead bitch, were attached to both sledges, first the front stake, then the back stake were knocked out. With wild shrieking and barking from dogs and people alike the charge was on!

Although the dogs were always harnessed about 100 yards apart, within the first 300 yards they inevitably converged and began a huge fight. I suppose that since they stood on a line all day long shouting abuse at each other there had to be retribution at some point. The handlers and the passengers would each be given a piece of black polythene pipe which they would use as truncheons as they waded in, grabbed hold of the fighting dogs and pulled the whole cacophony apart. They would then reorganise the dogs, untangle the harness and set off again.

There were never any more fights after that first fracas, and the teams operated beautifully. It was probably some of the best fun I've ever had, racing these sledge dogs over the tide crack where the sea ice met the land. Because of the tidal movement, the ice at the margin had cracks and fissures through it – some of them actually crevasses. As we flew over these humps and hollows dogs or people would occasionally disappear down a crevasse. This was not as dangerous as it sounds, for the dogs were all tied on, and in most cases the crevasses were relatively narrow so your shoulders stopped you going any further. Not far down the crevasses was exceedingly cold water, however, so it was a good idea not to fall too deeply in.

The veterinary problem that concerned the Antarctic Division most was arthritis amongst the dogs. English vets at their Halley Bay base had done quite a bit of research on arthritis, concentrating on taking

X-rays of hips and movies of the dogs' gait in an effort to understand why the disease was developing. Every leg joint I post-mortemed had an ulcerated arthritic lesion – the hips, stifles, hocks, even the joints between the toe bones showed up signs of these erosions on the surface of the cartilage. It was a relatively simple task to diagnose a condition called ostiochondritis descicans, a disease we see relatively frequently in breeds of large dogs in New Zealand.

The Scott Base huskies were descended from the dogs gathered by Sir Edmund Hillary and Harry Ayers when Hillary travelled across Antarctica to the South Pole to meet Sir Vivian Fuchs. I decided that the problem of arthritis lay in the rearing of the dogs, who performed best when they were given seal meat. The puppies were also fed seal meat as soon as they were weaned, with the result that their calcium requirements were totally neglected. As well, they were put in sledges at about six months old to begin their training, and once trained to pull they were left in the sledges to run with the adult dogs.

So the huskies' calcium levels were too low and the load on the bones excessive at too early an age. By feeding the puppies some calcium-rich, commercial puppy-rearing food and by drastically reducing their exercise, the arthritis disappeared.

Another problem confronting those responsible for the dogs in Antarctica was their poor fertility. The bitches came on heat every six months, but they didn't show the same signs as dogs in temperate climates. They bled briefly on the very first day of their heat, but showed no swelling at all, and seldom mated until seven to ten days after the first sign of heat and bleeding. In the city a bitch would bleed from the vagina on the first day and swell soon afterwards, remaining swollen for about three weeks. She would mate from about the tenth to the fourteenth day after the first sign of being on heat, and it would all be very obvious.

... giving birth to a very small litter in a temperature of about -10°C.

The situation with the Antarctic huskies was quite different. More often than not, someone would be sitting in the bar at the end of the day having a drink when he would look out to see that one of the bitches had escaped from the line and was being mated. Everyone would rush out and grab this bitch and tie her back on the line, without recording the date. This would be her only mating, resulting in her giving birth to a very small litter in a temperature of about -10°C. The pups would usually die, after which she would be put back on the line.

So once again this was a management problem. We observed and kept careful records of the bitches, anticipating when they would come on heat. When they did so they were mated on every second day for as long as they were receptive. Records were taken of the mating and as their pregnancy developed they were kept in an area called the cold porch, which was actually a big vehicle garage, where they could whelp away from the extremes of the Antarctic weather.

They then produced litters of eight or nine, as dogs of their size in New Zealand would do.

As part of my investigation into the dogs' fertility I collected semen from the male dogs. One of the visitors from Scott Base who used to come over and ring up his girlfriend from our post office – apparently it was cheaper than ringing from McMurdo – took a real interest in these activities and asked whether he could look down the microscope and see the sperm moving about.

He then astounded me by saying, 'I've often had doubts about my own fertility. Do you think if I gave you a sample we could have a look down the microscope?'

'I suppose that'd be okay,' I said.

I didn't see him for a few days, and hoped he'd forgotten about it. But he eventually turned up with his bottle in his pocket.

'It has to be recent,' I told him.

'Yes,' he said, looking a bit embarrassed. 'It is quite recent.'

So we put some drops on the microscope slide and I looked down. I could see some fat globules and a few cells that lined the tubes that deliver the sperm. There were some neutrophils, which are cells associated with infection, but no sperm.

I started to feel a bit uncomfortable at this stage. The thought that I might have to tell someone he was infertile, stuck as we were in this tiny spot in the most remote part of the world, was more than I could face so I carried on looking and looking, finally finding one deformed, dead sperm.

I turned the microscope on to its highest power and focused on this sperm. 'Well, you haven't got many,' I said, 'but they're truly enormous. If one of them got to the egg, I'm sure it would produce twins.'

He seemed to be happy with this explanation and I decided there and then that from now on I would stick resolutely to veterinary science.

During the examination of the bitches I had discovered that Lady, who was a seven- or eight-year-old malamute, had a lump in her groin. When I checked it more thoroughly I discovered to my horror that this was an inguinal hernia. Worse, the uterus had come through the hernia and within the uterus was a puppy, now far too big to go back through the hernia. The only option I had was to make the hernial ring bigger, replace the uterus and then repair the hernia – a major piece of surgery not to be undertaken lightly. In fact in all my years of practice, this was the first time I had ever experienced such a situation.

The dog handler and I went over to see the doctor at McMurdo, who turned out to be a lovely fellow who was keen to undertake the operation. Remarkably, he specialised in gynaecology – a bit frustrating for him in an all-male community. He was also keen on surgery. It later turned out that another reason for his enthusiasm was the fact that the anaesthetic machine they had been given had so far never been used, and he was pleased to get the chance to try it out on an animal before using it on a human.

So Lady was taken over to the operating theatre at McMurdo where we anaesthetised her, cleaned up the wound and draped it beautifully. It was a big day for the Americans, who had scrub nurses and theatre staff on hand. I was more than happy simply to assist with the surgery, and the doctor was more than happy to take charge. We made an incision through the skin and exposed the uterus and then enlarged the inguinal ring – not without difficulty, because there are some frighteningly big arteries running through this area – but everything went smoothly. The uterus was then replaced and the inguinal ring closed up so it wouldn't happen again. We performed the same operation on the other side as well, for it was possible that both sides might have been affected. The uterus hadn't actually gone through the other side, but it was still dilated enough for it to have done so. Lady went on to have three puppies about two days before I left, which was just lovely.

When my work had been completed the base commander suggested that we take both dog teams and some skidoos, which are little Volkswagen engine-powered snow-sledged tracked vehicles, to Scott's hut and Shackleton's hut, as well as count the Adelie penguins at the colony at Cape Royds. This was a true highlight. It was fantastic sitting on the sledge, sliding across the sea ice, with the only noise the scrunching of the tracks and the occasional farting of the dogs. Whenever they became thirsty the dogs just opened their mouths and dug their bottom jaws into the patches of softest snow, gathering mouthfuls as they loped along.

We reached Scott's hut by lunchtime. Entering both Scott's and Shackleton's huts turned out to be literally hair-raising experiences. The atmosphere was charged and, as you approached, you had the feeling that one of the early explorers would emerge out of the doorway and wave to you. On the exposed scoria outside Scott's hut were ruptured bags of barley, brought as food for the horses, that had remained there all these years, never germinating.

Inside, the bunkrooms still had the men's clothing – heavy serge trousers, socks, balaclavas and gloves – lying on the beds. Scott's cubicle also still had his clothing in it, while on the table in the main area of the hut was a partly dissected skua. The photographer's darkroom was filled with chemicals and equipment and the magnetic laboratory still had all its original equipment. A sheep's hindquarters, sheathed in mutton-cloth, hung in the corner of the room – no need for refrigeration here. Tins of Huntley & Palmers biscuits, still sealed, were stacked in the corner. The effect was uncanny.

We reached Shackleton's hut, where we planned to stay, at about four or five in the afternoon. The hut itself was similar to Scott's, except that on the back wall there was a big collection of horse harness, including horse crampons, bits and horseshoes with straps to enclose the hooves and with spikes on the bottom.

I became so interested in all this that later I researched the history of Scott and Shackleton and their use of horses. In Scott's case the horses proved to be useless. They could only pull their own food, which they refused to eat, and when they finally succumbed, the noble Englishmen wouldn't eat them. This was is in sharp contrast to Amundsen, whose dogs could pull far more than their own food, and who deliberately took sufficient spare dogs with him for them to be eaten to enable his party to get back home.

The other piece of history that fascinated me was the fact that several of the early explorers, certainly Shackleton and I think Mawson as well, became acutely ill after eating seal liver. They suffered from vitamin A poisoning, such as that we see in cats that eat a diet consisting solely of liver.

One thing we didn't see in the Antarctic huskies were internal parasites, or worms. This, of course, is because the worms – roundworms in dogs especially – are passed in the faeces, and the faeces from these dogs froze solid quite soon after they hit the ground. But we did see large numbers of worms in the 20 or so Weddell seals that were slaughtered each year both for scientific research and for dog food.

In the end it was this culling of the Weddell seals that sealed the fate of the huskies. Even though there was a steadily rising population of seals on the ice shelf, it was felt that the balance of the population was being artificially altered by this annual kill, and so a proper scientific approach could not be maintained.

Each year when I returned the face of Scott Base had changed subtly. New buildings went up, more mechanical gadgetry arrived, and the dogs became less valuable as transport. I suspect that they were never used as front-line transport, but what appeared to be overlooked was their marvellous entertainment and psychological value. Anyone feeling miserable and left out could go and sit with the dogs on the line, who were overjoyed to see anybody. The myth and theory was that if you patted one you had to pat them all, so you started at one end and worked your way along the whole row. The great thing was that even though they were absolutely vicious towards each other, they were very affectionate and loving towards humans.

I loved going out watch them. Each dog was attached to a line about six feet long which in turn was attached to the main steel wire. One of their favourite tricks after being fed was to place their piece of seal meat, often reduced by then to skin and fur and a little bit of fat, as far out as they could reach in one direction from the steel wire. They would then retreat as far as they could on the other side of the line, so they were about 12 feet from the bait, and pretend to go to sleep. Quite soon a skua would turn up to grab the seal meat and with one bound the husky would grab the skua and kill it. They never ate them, just killed them.

The only other time I saw the dogs hunting was when they were actually in the sledge coming home from Shackleton's hut. Ahead of us were two small Adelie penguins scooting along on their tummies. As soon as they saw the penguins the dog team veered ever so slightly off course until they could intercept them. Two of the dogs picked up these little Adelies in their mouths and carried them the way labradors carry ducks. The dog handler stopped the team and removed the penguins, who shook their feathers and hurried off, none the worse for wear.

On my last visit to the ice I was instructed by the Antarctic Division to euthanase all the dogs. They'd reached the end of their useful lives and they were to be disposed of. This was a very controversial decision, and by the time I arrived down there with Eric – poor, long-suffering Eric Saxby, the Field Operations Manager, who'd had his orders – there was open mutiny.

People were virtually sleeping with the dogs and when I turned up nearly everyone at Scott Base formed a great ring around the animals to stop anybody touching them. Eric called a conference that I chose not to attend. I was simply the executioner or, I hoped, not the executioner.

Finally a compromise was reached. Eric would have me examine every dog, and those that were too old and ill would be euthanased. That seemed a good decision, because out of the 13 or so dogs we only needed to put a couple down, so there were still enough for a dog team if necessary.

The following year all the dogs were sent home on an oil tanker, largely through the efforts of Bob McKerrow, a remarkable New Zealand adventurer, mountaineer and poet, who currently works for the Red Cross in Afghanistan. Bob heard about the dog problem and mortgaged his house to raise enough money to get the dogs shipped out.

The dogs weren't allowed to touch New Zealand soil, so they had to be crated on board the oil tanker and driven by truck to the closest airport before being flown to the States where, the idea was, they would form the nucleus of a team for an attempt at a trans-Antarctic expedition.

The last I heard, though, was that things hadn't gone too well. A chap from Anchorage told me that he'd heard that the dogs weren't doing very well in Colorado, so he'd checked them out and bought three of them himself, which he kept at home.

So that was the end of a long history of dogs at Scott Base. It was a sad occasion, meeting the tanker in Lyttelton and examining these dogs, each of whom I knew so very well, checking to make sure they were fit to be flown to the States. Once again I was instructed that any that were unsuitable were to be put down on the spot. Of course they were all passed as healthy.

9

A Home of our Own

After Faye and Arna moved into the little flat at Worcester Street, being available for emergencies at all hours wasn't as easy as it had been when I there by myself. Invariably we would be going somewhere when someone would arrive with a dog that had been run over and our evening would have to be cancelled. It seemed churlish to want to be on a roster when I lived above the clinic, so the only solution was to place myself at a distance from the clinic so that a roster became an equitable thing for all the people working at the practice.

It didn't take long – in fact it probably should have taken longer – for us to find a house. We thought it was charming. It was a flat-roofed, concrete house up Maffeys Road, which is one of the steepest roads in Christchurch.

We moved in with surprising ease. For people who had no concept of mortgages and finance, we seemed to fly through it. Maybe it was because our solicitor, Phil Davies, lived in the house below us and was quite keen to see some decent neighbours turn up, so things like mortgages and deposits were all very easily facilitated.

The house wasn't quite what we imagined it would be. It was

sound enough, apart from a big crack along the back wall. The engineer Phil asked to check on it said that because it was the same width all the way up, it was a settling crack and not due to subsidence – a distinction I found difficult to comprehend – but the upshot was that it was not a portent of the house's intention to slide down the hill. But in other respects as well the house was less than perfect. It had been designed and built by a potter. He had installed an enormous kiln in the basement under an equally large lounge and bar. The bedrooms were an afterthought. Faye was looking out the living room window one day when I was in the toilet. She heard the flushing of the toilet and soon afterwards saw a tide of water sweep across the clay driveway. This was the beginning of our renovations. Luckily not long afterwards a sewer was installed in Maffeys Road, and so the septic tank became unnecessary.

Over the years we replaced the old malthoid roof, we redesigned the kitchen, we altered the floor in the lounge and we carpeted the house. And then proceeded to have it gradually deteriorate. We reorganised the entrance at the front and added a garage. We laboriously built up a garden at the front. Adrian Turner and Nicky make a marvellous job of excavating, levelling, paving and retaining the back of the property. And over about two seasons – two fishing seasons, I might add – I built a deck that butted up to the house and ran along the front of the bedrooms to meet the kitchen. The idea for this started when the garage at the back of the house collapsed and the foundations seemed too handy not to use.

A year after we shifted into Maffeys Road Matthew was born. Despite the fact that Dr Sepp insisted on discussing the treatment for diarrhoea in his new kitten throughout, I found his birth an exhilarating and exalting experience. Calving cows and attending newborn kittens were minor events beside the birth of our own child.

The next day Faye's mother Etta, Arna and I were waiting expectantly beside the bed as the nurse came in carrying Matthew for his first feed from his mother.

'He's a strong healthy lad so I don't expect any trouble,' she said. 'But if you have any, don't hesitate to ring the bell. I'll leave you to it.'

Faye gingerly drew him toward her. I, with my experience of getting lambs to suckle, expressed some milk while Etta pushed the back of his head. Matthew began to cry. 'Let me do it on my own.' said Faye.

Arna, who already had the button in her hand, said, 'Let's ring the bell, Mum.'

Matthew was happily feeding and gaining weight the day we arrived in the hospital carpark with Arna's new pony in a float. We had discussed its purchase and negotiated grazing in the paddocks at the back of McCormick's Bay. With Faye's approval given from the hospital window as we paraded the pony around the carpark, Etta and I drove Arna and Goldie, as he was called, home for their first ride.

The horse had come complete with saddle and bridle. Arna seemed to know exactly how to assemble everything, so we stood back and watched. The pony seemed quite content to let Arna ride off on him to the distant corner of the paddock, but when they turned to trot home it broke into a full gallop interspersed with twists and bucks. As we watched, horrified, Arna fell off and with one foot stuck in the stirrup was dragged toward us with her helmeted head bumping on the ground. The pony swerved to avoid me as I ran forward and kept going until he reached the gate, where he stopped and began to graze.

Arna refused to admit to being either hurt or frightened and demanded another turn. Goldie and Arna resented my leading them but I flinched at the thought of having to tell Faye about anything more serious than what had already happened. Later, with the help of Faye's experience with horses, which was considerably more impressive than mine, Arna and Goldie agreed on an uneasy truce that lasted until she approached from behind one day when he was eating, and he kicked her and broke her leg.

All our pets have been given to us, except for one. One of the gifts was Sam the greyhound. Old Stan Gain, then in his seventies, was one of Christchurch's foremost greyhound trainers in the early days before greyhound racing became a commercial affair. He rang up in a panic one day to say that he had been walking with his two greyhounds tied to his wrists when they saw a cat and took after it, towing him along the road. Stan was very frail and no more than seven or eight stone. They caught the cat, which later escaped, but in the battle his best dog, called Cardigan Moss, had had its eye pierced by a claw.

Stan brought the dog in. The glassy part in the front of the eye had been torn clean through. There was a hole right through the cornea and the iris – the brown or yellow membrane immediately behind the cornea that alters its size to let the light in – was actually poking through the hole.

Luckily I had just been reading up on what to do with this sort of injury and I got to work. But I knew that it would be a disaster, this destroyed eye, if the operation didn't work. What you have to do is to flush the iris carefully out of the wound – the sooner you do it the better – then suture the corneal wound with the finest material available. You then put a needle in the side of the eye and, using either air or sterile water, reinflate the eye. Dogs have a third eyelid – a live bandage if you like – which you can sew across the front of the eye. This keeps the light out and the wound moist, while at the same time reducing the irritation and contributing generally towards the healing process.

When we finally took the stitches out and could see the wound, things had gone very well. The pupil worked perfectly, the scarring was minimal, and after we had given the dog some cortisone the scarring disappeared all together. This was a tremendous result, as the dog could keep on racing. In gratitude, Stan gave me Sam the greyhound – one of Cardigan Moss's pups.

To my astonishment Sam turned out to be one of the eight best racing greyhounds in New Zealand. Needless to say I didn't train him – there were enthusiastic people who were prepared to train greyhounds and Bill Gill, who trained Sam, did very well.

Greyhound racing had its beginnings in Christchurch in a small park in Marshlands, on Prestons Road. There was a mechanical hare that was frequently caught by the leading dog, and behind a scrim wall was the licensed booth from which operated the illegal bookie. A picnic atmosphere pervaded. There was hardly a New Zealand accent in the crowd and it was tremendous fun.

Sam's racing name was Beni Ulid, named by my father after an oasis he saw during the war. I'd turn up most Saturdays to watch the racing and be the vet on hand. Bill would normally put Sam in his box and be there at the end to retrieve him, but once he let me do it. I borrowed his white coat and proudly walked my dog past the crowd along the front straight to the boxes. I adjusted his cover, pushed him in and stood back. The hare came around, the doors opened and off they flew!

Sam was brilliant. He jumped out well, got to the rail position and flew around the course. He was beaten by a narrow margin and I was there to catch him and walk him back proudly past the crowd. I felt somewhat deflated, though, when a Scottish voice shouted, 'He'd have won if you'd taken his bloody collar off.'

One Christmas holidays, shortly after Matthew was born, trainer Bill phoned to say that he was going away and could we have Sam at our place. Of course I said yes, forgetting momentarily that we were about to set off on one of our own very rare family holidays. Then I remembered, and went home to tell Faye that instead of just the baby and Arna and Faye and me … well, instead of the baby and Arna and Faye and me and Kelly … there would also be Sam the greyhound coming to Akaroa.

Faye has developed a remarkable tolerance over the years to the vicissitudes of life with a vet, and seemed to handle it quite well until we started loading the car. Sam wandered around outside as we ferried food back and forwards from the kitchen to the car. At one point I noticed that he was looking a little fat, but it wasn't until Faye came out and found that Sam had eaten all the freshly-cooked meat that we were going to eat cold during the holiday, plus a fruit cake, that a sudden bout of post-natal depression seemed to strike my wife and she burst into tears.

Not being very good at consoling people in tears, I decided to throttle the greyhound instead. The screams of the dog combined with the tears and shrieks of Faye only ceased when neighbours started to come out of their houses and stare at us in the driveway.

Both Faye and Sam seemed unusually subdued on the way over to Akaroa, and things didn't brighten up when we heard a small noise and realised that Sam had squirmed his way into the bassinet on top of the baby.

The mood of the holiday was somewhat tarnished by these events, and the two weeks in Akaroa seemed to pass very slowly. Each day we would allocate walking duties – someone to wheel the baby and someone to hold the dog. When we got back to Christchurch Sam was banished outside, along with the pet lamb that we had also recently acquired. The only way to keep the pet lamb out of the house was to put a barricade at the bottom of the stairs that led into the house. This barricade was so effective that people were unable to use the stairs either, so we put a ladder up beside the staircase for people to come and go.

One Sunday morning shortly after our return we were sleeping in when the phone rang. It was a neighbour from up the hill, Tahu Fenton, to say that his neighbour's cat looked very sick and could I see it straightaway. Normally when I get calls like this I tell people to go down to the clinic, but seeing it was so sick and so close by it seemed only reasonable to have a look. The cat's owner arrived about five minutes later, before I could get dressed, so I pulled on a towelling dressing-gown and looked over the edge of the stairs to see him standing below with a cat box. I climbed down the ladder, opened the box and reported that the cat was dead.

'I'm glad my wife's not here,' he said. 'She would be so distraught.' At that moment his wife came up the path. I passed on the bad news to her, and she was truly distraught, falling to the ground on her knees and sobbing bitterly. At this moment Sam the greyhound seized his chance and mounted her from behind. I kicked the greyhound firmly up the backside, which in retrospect might have been a mistake, and scurried back up the ladder inside. As I reached the top I could see her white face staring aghast at me. I felt somehow that I had momentarily lost the standard of professionalism normally required of a vet.

Despite my liberal habits, I've always been very conscientious about not having a drink until the work's finished. So it was with some diffidence that I accepted a glass of champagne from Mrs Spiers, even if the occasion did warrant something of a celebration. Mrs Spiers' bitch had just given birth to three pups – not an unusual occurrence in itself, but these pups had begun life as a semen specimen in England. The semen had been frozen and transported to New Zealand in liquid nitrogen, where it had sat for five to six months in the fridge till the bitch had come on heat again, because the first time the plane had arrived too late. We inseminated the semen surgically, opening the uterus up and injecting the semen straight into the uterus. Lo and behold, Dido gave birth to three dalmatian pups – the first time this procedure had ever been done in New Zealand.

We felt pretty proud of this, so I accepted both the champagne and one of the pups. His name was Rallygig of Farley Green, and he arrived at about the same time as Bridget, the second of our children, came home from the nursing home. So Bridget and Gig grew up together. Life wasn't always easy with two young children plus Gig the dalmatian, for he turned out to be one of these problem dogs.

I freely acknowledge that my training was inadequate – I was used to a little dog like Kelly, who actually trained me rather than the reverse. But Gig was a big, boisterous dalmatian who needed lots of training, domination and willpower, as well as time. But I worked for 50 or 60 hours a week, so Gig was expected to train himself.

Which he did. He became proficient at getting out and running away, and he became even more proficient at getting into fights. In desperation I took him jogging one day. It's not a regular pastime of mine, jogging, so after 100 yards or so I hit the wall, as they say, starting to slow down and get a bit unco-ordinated. At this point

Bridget and Gig arrived at about the same time.

Gig ran across in front of me and down I went, skinning both my knees and my elbow.

Gig left, dragging the lead. I fondly thought he was going to go and get help, but he didn't come back for three days. He was seen in the company of several rough dogs and between them they must have sought out every bitch on heat throughout the eastern suburbs of Christchurch. He came home scarred, battered and exhausted but smiling.

Gig's worst enemy was Phil Davies' dog Brandy, who lived right next door. Brandy and Gig would have a fight about once a week. I think they enjoyed it, but it used to upset both sets of owners. Phil's wife, Alison, would dash out with her hockey stick and beat the dogs up – well actually she only used to beat Gig up, but it did help to separate them.

Mrs Spiers was quite emphatic that Gig remain a male dog, in case he was needed for stud work, and he did have three successful matings.

But when he reached middle age I implored Mrs Spiers to let me castrate him because I thought it would reduce his fighting.

It did. He stopped fighting overnight, but unfortunately that part of his brain that had been busy keeping a diary of where bitches were and when they came on heat was now taken up with knowing when the rubbish would be put out. He toured Christchurch ripping open rubbish bags – no doubt in revenge for having been castrated.

One of the neighbours down below was a particularly fussy school teacher and, while I admit that having your rubbish bag ripped open on a regular basis is a frustrating experience, I used to resent the way he would come to our place at about 6.30 in the morning and insist that I bring my own rubbish bag down to his house to pick up his rubbish – smelly old rotten cabbages, soiled babies' nappies, the whole variety of unmentionable things that go into rubbish bags. It was a salutary experience, but I continued to feel very resentful.

Gig's one real attribute was that he was a good blood donor. By the time he reached middle age he had quietened down sufficiently for me take him to the clinic and sit him on the table, put a needle in his jugular vein and collect a bag of blood without a great deal of fuss. One night I had to perform a caesarean on a bitch at about 11pm. By 1 o'clock we had finished the surgery but the dog looked a little pale so I put her on a drip. The circulation often fails a little in anaesthetised dogs, especially bitches after the volume of their pups has been suddenly removed, so it's not uncommon for them to need a drip.

The bitch's owner, however, was concerned that we might need blood, in spite of the fact that only a small amount of blood had actually been lost. But things have a habit of backfiring if you go head to head in conflict with an owner's wishes, so at 1.15 in the morning I went home and brought back Gig, sat him on the table, got the bag of blood, connected it up to the little bitch and sat back to watch. Of course she didn't really need the blood, and at that hour of the morning I found myself becoming quite cross.

As I attended the dog I watched out of the corner of my eye as Gig wandered around the room. He sauntered over to the woman's handbag that she had left lying on the floor, and – it was almost as though I had willed him to do it – cocked his leg and passed a steady stream of yellow urine straight into the open bag. It seemed to go on for ever, and soon the purse got so full that her post office savings book floated out the top. I just looked upwards and thought that maybe there was some justice in the world after all.

Gig lived until he was about 14 – much older than the average for dalmatians. I was convinced that it was sheer perversity that kept him alive. Finally one morning he was unable to get up. He'd had quite bad arthritis for a long time – in fact Arna had run over him once in the car, and that seemed to improve him. But eventually the arthritis, combined probably with some spinal cord compression from a disc, paralysed him. So I was quite grateful to be able to say finally, 'Goodbye, Gig, I haven't totally enjoyed your life – but some aspects of it certainly made me laugh.'

Our pet magpie, on the other hand, was pure joy. It had a broken leg when it was brought in by a schoolboy, so I said we'd put a pin in it and look after it at home until it could fly, when I'd release it.

The magpie hobbled around the house and made itself totally at home. It would cuddle up to Lucy the old dog, another member of our small menagerie, pluck her whiskers and squawk until she allowed it to curl up inside her legs so it could bask in the warmth of her fluffy coat. As it grew older it would go to sleep on the back of the couch.

Faye's mother Etta, who's a very tidy and house-proud person, arrived for a holiday and was aghast to discover this magpie sitting beside her on the couch. She soon became quite fond of it in a nervous sort of way, but it really upset her composure when it squirted a great dollop of white poop down the back of the couch. The fact that no one immediately jumped up to clean up the mess probably worried her more!

Etta was aghast to discover this magpie sitting beside her on the couch.

I was watching the magpie one day when it waddled across the floor to a sunny patch and suddenly fell over on its back. My God, I thought, it's died! It just lay there with its feet in the air and both wings spread out. But I soon realised that it was breathing; in fact it was perfectly conscious and comfortable. It was sun-bathing! Often after that we would see it lying in the sun, flat on its back with its wings spread out.

I took the pin out after about three or four weeks and the bone healed very well, but the bird refused to leave. As soon as it had learnt to fly it would go touring around the neighbourhood, picking up delicacies. One of our immediate neighbours took a special shine to it and would feed it garlic steak and paint its toenails red. The fledgling magpie would come flying back holding a piece of steak and trying to work out the correct trajectory to land on the railing of the deck still holding on to the steak in its beak. Often it would just crash onto the lawn and then hold the steak in its beak as it walked up the steps to the house.

One day it was sitting on the balcony when a large, beautiful, black and white magpie, immaculately clean and formally dressed, flew down and sat beside it. From then on they toured the neighbourhood together, until one day the pair of them flew straight between a group of us as we sat on the deck, in a sort of a fly-past. And that was the last we ever saw of old Maggots.

Soon after that one of the neighbours came in with a cat that had been wounded and insisted that our magpie had ripped a great hole in it. She wanted the surgery for nothing. I was able to tell her that the magpie had since reverted to the wild and was not ours any more, and I charged her the full amount.

Faye's forbearance with the veterinary things I did, and do, is legendary, and once – only once – was she rewarded. I'd been called out to see some puppies – these were very precious puppies – whose owner had been struggling to get the mother to feed them. She had been feeding them herself for the last five days, but finally she had to sleep. When she woke up she found that they were cold and nearly lifeless, so she was desperate. Would I please look after them?

I knew how much effort had been put into producing these pups – there'd been long courses of drug treatment and considerable expense before we succeeded in getting the bitch to conceive. So I had to agree. We weren't equipped with incubators and humidifiers and modern equipment to rear puppies, so the best I could do was to take them home, put them into our bed beside Faye, crawl in beside them and hope I didn't roll over.

It worked quite well. Every hour or so they would wake up and cry, and I would wake up and feed them, and Faye would wake up and complain – but they survived. And they went on to become show winners, which was the intention in the first place.

Early one morning about a month later the telephone rang. It was a radio station that was holding, as a promotion, a series of thank-you prizes. People could ring to nominate someone as a way of showing their gratitude for something that had been done for them. And we, apparently, had won an evening at Tiffany's restaurant.

10

Leaving Maffeys Road

One of the problems that Maffeys Road posed was in the maintenance and upkeep of cars. The road climbed a very steep hill and, for some reason, starting a car and going down the hill with the motor cold seemed to do things to head gaskets and brakes. Faye's green Mini, which she regarded as her dowry, was the first to suffer serious problems. The brakes hadn't been working properly for about a week so I said I would take the car to the garage on the way to work. I backed out of the drive and started off down the hill – much faster than I anticipated. Reason seemed to desert me at this stage. I used the foot-brake: nothing happened. I used the hand-brake: nothing happened. I worked out that I would have to drive the car into the bank or I would be in big trouble; it was accelerating at a furious pace by now. The only driveway on Maffeys Road that did not leave at right angles was near the bottom of the hill and belonged to the unfortunate school teacher, the owner of Gig's rubbish bags. So I chose that one. I flew between the garage and the house, missing both. They had a retaining wall overlooking their front lawn, screened by small trees. One of those small trees slowed my descent slightly as I hurtled over the wall. I could see the estuary revolving in front of the windscreen and imagined that the little car would end up rolling on its side and crashing through the front hedge, when suddenly it jolted a little bit and descended smoothly onto the front lawn to park parallel with the retaining wall. Well, smoothly wasn't quite the right word: the wheels were splayed out at odd angles. The only damage to me was a small cut on my chin. I picked up my lunch, looked up at the house – apparently everyone had gone to work – and I walked back up the hill to explain to Faye.

After my 404 Peugeot wore out a bit I replaced it with what I anticipated and dreamed was to be the perfect car – a 504 automatic Peugeot. But I was sadly disappointed. The motor overheated all the time and it had very little power. One autumn the council decided to do some minor alterations at the bottom of Maffeys Road. Soon after they started it rained solidly for two weeks and so the whole bottom segment of the road fell off into the estuary. The result was that for a long period, while retaining walls were being formed, the only exit from our place was uphill. With Gallic pique, the Peugeot refused to make this trip in cold blood, so each morning I had to resort to going down the hill to an open area where the road flattened to begin my ascent.

Most mornings I could manage, but this particular morning the car, in a foul temper, absolutely refused to get going. I warmed the motor up and started up the hill only to have it die after about 30 or 40 yards. I then glided back down with the car in neutral to my level spot and tried again. On the fourth try it was my turn for a fit of temper. Deciding to teach this car a lesson, I put my foot flat on the accelerator and held it there. 'I'm going to thrash the daylights out of this motor,' I thought, and that's exactly what happened. After about three or four minutes of high-pitched screaming there was a terrible clattering noise and some important part of the motor disintegrated. The vehicle had to be retrieved by a salvage operator and taken to the garage.

Our house overlooked the estuary which, at high tide every weekend was covered in yachts. We watched this glorious sight for several years before we realised it would be a good idea to have a go ourselves. A friend on the West Coast had an old Cherub that he said we could have for $100. On the way over Arthur's Pass the side of the yacht rubbed on the tyre so when it arrived the plywood had a gaping hole in it.

We spent the whole winter repairing the boat and sanding it down, smoothing the bottom beautifully so it would glide effortlessly through the water, belying the fact that it was about 50 pounds over the average weight for this type of boat. My friend Bruce Ansley had some knowledge of sailing and offered to join forces with me. Jerome K. Jerome, I think, would have felt comfortable in our company as we pottered and fossicked and fussed about our elderly yacht.

It took a long time to master even the rudimentary skills of sailing the thing, but we finally had the main jib and spinnaker both working at the same time. With Bruce hiking out over the side, attached to the top of the mast by the trapeze wire, we skimmed on a wild broad reach across an estuary easterly. This thrilling event lasted for about 150 yards until we hit a sand bank. Bruce performed a sort of maypole act around the mast to land in the water with the boat sinking on top of him. The impact on the centre board had wrenched the bottom out of the boat.

After another winter of repairs and maintenance we were ready for the next yachting season and sufficiently confident to enter our first competitive race. Our excitement at not coming last was dampened when, at the second mark, Bruce noticed that the boat seemed to be going much more slowly than usual – we were actually being lapped by some of the leading boats – and we seemed to be sitting a bit lower in the water. It was only when it finally gurgled beneath the tide, leaving just the pointed bow visible, that we realised that we'd forgotten to put the bungs in. Alas, the weight of the water in the various compartments of the old boat caused further damage as the rescue boat towed us back, so the wreckage that was finally dragged up the slipway was beyond help. It was time for a new boat.

Undaunted by this small lapse in seamanship I decided to take command of an expedition to navigate the uncharted waters of the Bay of Islands. When I phoned to book I offered the information that my sailing experience was restricted to Cherubs. I omitted to mention that the said boat was no longer sailable. The owner thought that I had quite enough experience for one of his boats and asked me to forward a large deposit.

The hand-picked crew of Faye, moderately pregnant with Bridget, Arna with a broken leg and Matthew, who at two was able to walk quite confidently, embarked on a Noelex trailer yacht from Paihia. The first day was marred only by the breakage of the main halyard, the rope that travels up the hollow centre of the mast to hoist the mainsail. But as Matthew had fallen off the table and Arna began to feel seasick when the boat heeled under the mainsail, I was quite happy to do without it anyway.

Landfall was achieved by running aground as we ran before the wind under the jib. By morning the boat was 50 yards from the nearest water and lying on its side. We used this opportunity to rethread the halyard and by winding up the centre board we were able to return to level and have a meal off the table. By early afternoon we were in 18 inches of water and still stuck. Faye became mutinous when, after trying to push the boat free on my own and failing, I asked her to help. Her particular objection was my reasoning that by helping she would be doing two things. First she would be adding valuable horsepower to the push and secondly by leaving the boat she would lighten it markedly. Her outburst was renewed when, after we refloated the boat and proved me correct, she accused me of standing on her fingers as I scrambled back aboard.

With an improvement in the skills of the crew in the following days we were able to explore most of the inlets and islands. We even sailed up the river into Kerikeri for a restaurant meal and a shower in the changing rooms under the grandstand.

On the last day, as we were sailing back to Paihia to return the yacht, the wind got up. The sea, initially an attractive cobalt blue, turned a malevolent turquoise. The waves began as a swell, then steepened and finally spray was being blown from their tops by the screaming wind. It was calmer under the hills but when the outboard gave up we were unable to steer around the rocks. In the end we sailed straight downwind with only a handkerchief of jib unfurled. As it was we hurtled across the harbour, through an area that the chart showed as having many dangerous submerged rocks, broadsided into the marina and slammed sideways into our mooring post.

It was too rough to row ashore so we slept the night on board. Any thoughts we had had of sailing around the world vanished on that day.

Bridget was born a few months later. She had gold hair and an elfish, serene, wise face. The aversion to water that the yachting holiday produced in me seemed not to have passed on to her. She loved water. Many of the photos we have depict her in it, paddling, splashing, laughing.

When she was three she drowned. She was face down in the water when I found her, her red-gold hair moving gently over her back, her skin translucent. When I began mouth-to-mouth resuscitation her stomach blew up. When I pushed on her stomach she vomited. I rolled her over and began artificial respiration by moving her arms as I'd learned at school. A small puddle of water formed beneath her mouth. The thought that it took such a small amount to drown someone stayed with me. The ambulance and the doctor appeared. In the ambulance they kept saying to me, 'Can you feel the pulse in her neck?' I think they thought I was the doctor.

Faye and I were left alone in a small room at the hospital. After ten minutes I said to Faye, 'I think she's dead.' They came and told us they had been unable to save her and asked, 'Would you like to see her?' The hospital is a busy place and so quite soon another emergency took their attention. They had to ask us to leave Bridget behind. We stood on the footpath holding each other in the rain and waiting for a taxi.

Every day we visited Bridget at the chapel. Matthew, fortunately, was too young to be fully aware of what was happening and was more interested in watching the ducks swimming in the pond through the open window. By the third day her hair had started to fall out and the make-up had begun to clot. She was becoming a bizarre charade, a garish mannikin. Her favourite toys were placed in her tiny white coffin.

Matthew didn't go to the funeral. We asked if he would like to give one of his toys. He said, 'You're not throwing that down the hole as well.'

After Bridget's death a hopelessness descended on the family. We, in attempting to quash our grief, managed to obliterate every emotion other than anger – the only one to survive. After a life of antiseptic atheism I reinvented a belief in God. Not that I wanted salvation. I needed someone powerful to direct my hatred at. I would stand on the back lawn at night, staring at the sky and cursing God. It didn't help. I would begin to do some gardening and end up sitting crumpled, surrounded by cigarette butts. The only time I could still function was at work. Amazingly I would smile and chat and listen to other people's worries and be sympathetic. As soon as I arrived home I would sit in a chair and smoke until I fell asleep.

The only time the facade cracked at work was when a woman came in with her daughter, whom I knew to have been born within a day or two of Bridget. She asked, naturally, how my daughter was. I could not avoid saying that she had died. It was the only time I was reduced to tears at work.

I became acutely sensitive to other people's worries. I knew the pain of someone telling me that the cat in front of us belonged to her dead husband, or that this dog was a living memory of a dead daughter. I became a hall of mirrors distorting the shell that remained of me to reflect the image that people wanted to see of themselves in me. Inside I was dead.

Four years ago we shifted from Maffeys Road – about ten years too late. At the end it had become a tomb that we were all likely to die in. From that point on the spirits of the family lifted. A terrible period of our lives was over.

11

Out on Our Own

For Murray, Barbara, Faye and me, setting up our own practice and moving to Aldwins Road was an exciting stage in our lives. We had dissolved the partnership with Roy, in itself a painful, stressful experience for Roy as well as for us, and we have some regrets about how it was all managed.

The house on the corner of Marlborough Street and Aldwins Road was old. It would perhaps have been less expensive if we had bulldozed it to the ground and built our clinic from scratch, but we didn't have the money then and we don't have the time now.

At one point during the reconstruction I looked in the window and thought to myself, 'What on earth have we done?' It was stripped of any lining; its three fireplaces had all been removed, leaving gaping holes in the roof, the ceiling and the walls.

But the final result proved successful after the interior had been totally re-lined and painted. The lino-layer was still at work when we opened, so people had to step over the top of him to enter. And hordes of them poured in. It was like the early days of Worcester Street.

When Robin Harrison of 3ZB invited me to be the radio vet on his talkback show I was delighted, as this seemed to be a great opportunity to promote our new clinic. But I did very poorly. The questions I had no difficulty with at all at the clinic were almost impossible to deal with over the radio. Most of the discussions ranged around dog behaviour or cat behaviour and all the animal illnesses I was most familiar with were hardly ever mentioned.

One woman asked me, 'Why does my cat spray inside?'

'Normally the cat would spray to cover the urine of a tom cat that had got into the house,' I said.

'I see. Actually it only ever sprays on my boyfriend's underpants.'

Someone wanted to know why her dog kept eating its own faeces. 'It's a bad habit,' I replied. 'Try putting Tabasco sauce on its faeces.'

'He eats it straight after he does it.'

'Well, stand behind him with the sauce bottle when he does it.'

Robin shook his head at me. These were not the sorts of answers he wanted. I tried to do better. The next caller complained that her dog had bad breath. Foolishly I found myself being drawn into a no-win situation.

'Have you tried cleaning his teeth?'

'Yes, I clean them all the time. Besides she's a girl.'

I apologised, and went on. 'Some breeds, spaniels for instance, have folds down the sides of their bottom lips that get food and saliva stuck in them.'

'She's not a spaniel.'

'How about a change of diet? Sometimes the smell comes from their stomachs.'

'I've done that,' she said.

I went on down the list, mentioning lungs, sinus infections and tonsils, with each suggestion being firmly, triumphantly, rejected.

Finally I said in exasperation, 'Do you think your dog licks its bum?'

She hung up just as Robin was struggling to cut me short. That was the last time I was invited to speak on the radio.

Bill Robinson had been a farmer before he came to town. He had the traditional farmer's disdain for vets until the fateful day when his best stud dog pulled the skin off its penis. The look on Bill's face was one of pure horror as he brought the dog in in his arms. He'd wrapped its whole abdomen in a sheet as much to prevent him seeing what had happened as to give the dog comfort.

'You won't believe what's happened, Doc,' he said. 'Look, he's pulled the whole skin off his cock.'

'How did that happen, do you think?'

'I had him tied to that bitch of mine – it was time for another litter. There's a rottie living next door and whenever they see one another it's always a bit of a hullabaloo. I don't know how it happened, but the bloody rottie got out and came into our yard just as my dog was in the middle of mating the bitch. He took one look at the rottie and off he went after him, dragging the poor bitch behind him. The next thing he came out with a bloody sucking noise and got stuck straight into the rottie and grabbed it by the throat. The rottie took off home yelping and carrying on, but when the dust had settled you couldn't believe it. There's this bloody big thing hanging off my dog's sheath, like taking a sock off. He's pulled the whole bloody skin off his penis.'

With the dog anaesthetised, I discovered that it was exactly as Bill had described. From behind the bulbar urethral glands – the organs that swell up at the base of the penis when a dog ties – the surface of his penis had been pulled completely away. It was only attached by the tip where the urethra forms a tube down the inside of the penis.

By turning this sock of skin back to its correct position and putting stitches in where the torn edges had met, we were able to save it.

'See here,' I said to Bill Robinson. 'The blood supply comes from the base of the penis but also from the urethra at the tip. If you're unlucky you lose the blood supply and the whole lot sloughs,' I warned. 'so keep him away from bitches for the next ten days. I don't want him getting an erection.'

We were lucky. The skin healed beautifully without even a scar and Bill's attitude towards vets changed drastically. He became a passionate disciple. Nothing was done without veterinary advice.

Over the years Bill became a prominent breeder of boxers and together we produced some very nice pups. Subtly, I thought, I suggested methods that might improve the breeding of his dogs; subtly, he thought, Bill ignored me.

After the appalling accident to his dog's penis, Bill decided that artificial insemination was the answer. This became a regular routine at the clinic. Collection of semen from male dogs is not very difficult; they are often more than willing to part with it. We use a funnel-shaped plastic envelope with a tube fitted into the bottom end, which is held in the palm of the vet's hand and pushed over the dog's erect penis. Most dogs fail to become the slightest bit interested unless they have a bitch on heat standing in front of them, but Bill's dog, after two or three episodes, associated the clinic with the ejaculation of semen. In fact he would stand in the carpark in full view of the 27,000 cars a day that drove past, and begin his preparatory stimulation, humping gently as he walked towards the front door.

I was always a little disconcerted by Bill's habit of bringing his grandchildren along to watch. They would stand there with their noses inches away from the action and when, after the semen had been collected, we checked it under a microscope, Bill would lift these pre-schoolers up so they too could see the magnified sperm swirling past. We then put a long pipette into the bitch's vagina, right up to the cervix, and injected the semen from a syringe. Bill would invariably say to his grandchildren, 'Look dears, see the sperm going in!'

We found that caesareans were of great benefit when Bill's boxers gave birth. The puppies' squat, flat faces and the bitches' narrow pelvises made normal whelping quite difficult, and more often than not we lost more than half the litter while the bitch struggled over a 24-hour period to produce her puppies.

Bill would write down the mating date and we would check that the bitch was pregnant. As time went by we could then use the ultra-sound to measure the pups' heads, which gave us a reasonably accurate indicator of when she was going to whelp.

Bill became increasingly enthusiastic about this procedure. His pups were valuable, so the surgery costs were easily absorbed, and we could easily arrange the right date so that with all the full-time staff on everything would proceed very smoothly.

I don't know how he did it, but one day Bill got it wrong. Perhaps he wrote the date down wrongly, but he discovered to his horror that his bitch had started to whelp at about 10 o'clock at night, several days early. He rang the vet on duty, an Australian woman who had been doing a locum for us for several months. 'I need Dave's home number,' he said. 'I've got trouble with my bitch.'

'Sorry, you can't have it,' she said. 'He's not on duty.'

'Oh, he won't mind if I ring,' said Bill.

'No,' she said. 'He's over on the Coast, fishing. What's wrong?'

'My bitch is having pups and she needs a caesar.'

'Okay, bring her straight down,' said the vet, who was very experienced and very capable. When Bill arrived she examined the dog and said, 'Yes, no question, we'll need to do a caesarean straight-away.'

Bill got cold feet. He decided that because it wasn't me he wasn't going to have a caesarean and, even though the locum insisted, he said, 'No, give her an injection and I'll take her home.'

So she did. At 5 o'clock in the morning he rang back to say that he had two dead pups, one was stuck. Could the vet help? So at six in the morning the bitch finally got her caesarean, producing one more dead pup. The whole thing had been a tragedy.

Bill, consumed with guilt and grief, decided he would have nothing more to do with the whole business. He brought the dog into me and said, 'Put it down.' When we sent the bill for the caesarean he refused to pay. We took the matter to the small claims court and he claimed that the vet had refused to do a caesarean and as a consequence all the pups had died.

The adjudicator believed us and insisted that Bill pay, but the whole thing proved very distressing for an intelligent, sensitive vet who had not been in practice long enough to be cynical.

'I don't mind my colleagues criticising me – at least they have the knowledge to do so – but I can't understand how clients feel they can criticise me,' she said.

'Sadly, they are the only ones who ever will,' I replied.

Vince Peterson had a list that he called his Rules of Practice. These were a fairly undefined group of veterinary words of wisdom because he was always adding to them. I can remember two of them.

'Some live, some die and some things never change,' went the first.

The second, cynical but surprisingly accurate, was: 'If they can pay, it's not parvo.'

Parvovirus is a gastro-intestinal disease of dogs that arrived in New Zealand as a result of a world-wide epidemic in the mid -1970s. It spread throughout the world so fast that it was rumoured to be an unwanted passenger in a dog vaccine. The disease is devastating to susceptible dogs, producing vomiting, diarrhoea and dehydration. To begin with the discharge is very watery and profuse, making nursing difficult, and later it becomes blood-tinged, finally turning into pure blood. Untreated the dog will die in one to three days. Only young dogs are affected and for some reason the disease becomes worse in the summer. Vaccination confers very good protection, and this is the reason that puppies owned by people with little money are the most likely to be affected.

One day, just as I was leaving Aldwins Road after finishing a Saturday morning clinic, keen to get home and listen to the rugby, a car turned into the carpark. To be more accurate, it lurched into the carpark and came to halt against the brick wall. In fact it knocked some of the wall down. The driver struggled out over the rubble of the wall and staggered around to the passenger side He opened the door and bent down to pick his dog up from the floor in front of the seat but was prevented from doing so by the passenger, a young woman who seemed to be remarkably drunk, falling out onto the footpath.

She wore a leather microskirt, black fishnet stockings with huge holes in them, no shoes, a black lace top and, as far as I could tell as she lay on the ground, absolutely no underwear at all. Together they lurched into the clinic, holding their sickly little dog, who was gently leaking bloody diarrhoea over her fishnet stockings.

'Do you think you can save him, Doctor?' she asked. 'We don't care what it costs.'

That last phrase tends to be particularly jarring to people like me, because in most cases the clients who truly don't care what it costs have no intention whatsoever to pay. But as I looked at her with her tears, scum-laden with mascara and starting to obscure the small star tattooed on her cheek, I realised that beneath her maudlin, drunken demeanour she genuinely loved this little dog. When sober she would grieve seriously if he died.

'Of course I can try,' I said, kicking myself.

To my surprise things went spectacularly well. We have developed a policy of intensively treating these dogs with intravenous fluid therapy, giving them a blood transfusion that provides antibodies against parvo along with clotting factors and in many cases this can produce a very good result. We kept the little dog for treatment at the clinic and each day one or both of them would visit.

The man apologised for the impression they had given on their first visit and they both helped the nurses with the baths needed every time the puppy passed more bloody diarrhoea and found itself too weak to shift out of it. Eventually it stopped vomiting and they were there to offer it its first meal. As soon as it could eat and keep its food down we let them take the dog home. I really thought I had made the right decision for once when much to my surprise and delight I was paid fully by a cheque in the mail.

About a week later the cheque came back, referred to drawer. When I rang the number that had been given I was again surprised to find that it was current and that it did indeed belong to the people who had brought the dog in. So rather than be aggressive and rude I started by asking how the puppy was.

'Just great,' he said. 'It's bouncing around all over the place.'

This seemed too good an opportunity to miss. 'Funny you should say that,' I replied. 'So's your cheque.'

In contrast it was always pleasure to see someone like Dr Sparrow coming through the front door. He was a softly-spoken, gentle man with greying hair, unlike his dog Ben who was noisy, over-active and black – about what you'd expect from a labrador. When Ben was young, his owner and I speculated on when he might quieten down, and I reasoned that three or four would be a reasonable age, but he finally settled down to a more measured pace at about ten, when the arthritis in his back legs got so bad he couldn't rear up.

Ben's favourite trick when he came to see me was to advance on me, grab me with his front legs somewhere between my waist and my neck, and then try to mount me. Such affection is gratifying, but if taken too far it can be a bit embarrassing.

His major complaint over all these years was his ear infections. He had a chronic, low-grade – sometimes more severe – yeast infection, which we treated periodically with antifungal drugs. On one occasion his ears became so bad that I said I thought they smelt like blue vein cheese.

Dr Sparrow returned with Ben two weeks later to check on progress we'd made, so I asked how were the ears?

'Oh, definitely better now, definitely better,' he said. 'They smell much more like Stilton now. Far better quality.'

Mark lived on a high-country farm about two hours from Christchurch which was covered in snow for a good part of the winter. Apart from running his farm dogs he was developing a group of malamutes, which he trained as sledge dogs. One of them, Clara, had accidentally mated with his farm dog, so he'd taken her to the local vet for a 'mismate' injection. Once upon a time mismate injections were quite safe and seldom gave any trouble. Then Stilboestrol, the hormone that was used for mismates, was taken off the market and replaced by another drug called Oestradiol.

That was when the trouble started, for giving a bitch Oestradiol as a mismate injection in a large single dose, just as the dog's own progesterone levels start to rise after ovulation, sometimes produces a side-effect called pyometra, in which the uterus fills with mucus and becomes infected. Artificial hormone alterations are the real villains behind this disease. In most cases this is the end of the dog's breeding career, as surgical removal of the uterus is advised.

Sadly, Mark's dog Clara, who was scheduled to become the foundation of his breeding stock, developed pyometra, so he decided to bring her to Christchurch to see us. We were able to show by X-ray and ultrasound that the uterus had pus in it and that she was not pregnant; in fact Clara had a closed pyometra – the cervix was not allowing the pus to escape. Recently we had been following a treatment programme using a drug called prostaglandin, which induces the cervix to dilate and the uterus to contract, thus expelling the pus. But even then the chance of the bitch getting in pup after this regime was only 30 to 40 per cent if she has a closed pyometra.

We treated Clara with daily injections of prostaglandin and antibiotics. For six days nothing happened. The white cell count stayed high, indicating that there was still a rampant infection present, while the uterus still appeared swollen and fluid-filled on the ultrasound. But on the seventh day everything changed. We arrived at the clinic to find Clara with great gobs of mucus around the cage floor – a real breakthrough. After another five days of treatment she went home with a month's supply of antibiotics and a warning to Mark that next time she came on heat she was likely to have a recurrence of the condition, even without another injection of hormone.

Mark rang about two months later to say that she was back on heat well before she was due. 'I know it's a bit early to mate her but I want to try out a young dog I've just imported from Australia.'

So I wished him luck and sent down some more antibiotics. About three weeks later he rang to say that he thought the pyometra was back. 'Can you fit her in today?'

'You set off now and I'll wait for you.'

It was too early to see any changes on the ultrasound, but the blood count was starting to rise again. It looked as though the problem was coming back. We changed the antibiotics and treated Clara for another ten days.

'Cross your fingers. Is it pus or puppies?' I said, holding the probe over Clara's freshly shaved abdomen. This was her 28th day, when pregnancy is most easily detected. And there on the ultrasound were these beautiful spherical foetuses, each with its heart beating and no sign of any infection at all.

Mark was ecstatic. 'You don't realise how important this result is to me. That young dog I used got in a fight a week ago and was killed. He only had one bite hole in his neck when I found him, but he was stone dead. So now I've got his replacement. I can't believe my luck.'

'The other good thing,' I replied, 'is that now she's pregnant you've eliminated the risk of pyometra. She's at no greater risk than any other dog.'

Mrs Fraser's little shih tzu was a chronic aborter. She had been pregnant three times and lost all her puppies. Despite our advice and her better judgment, Mrs Fraser took her to Australia for a mating. We did our ultrasound pregnancy check at 28 days and there were four puppies, each with its heart beating away happily.

We checked the shih tzu again at seven weeks and they all looked well, still growing normally, but suddenly with a week to go the bitch aborted, passing a pile of macerated tissue and pus. Once again it looked as though we'd failed.

'Let me just do another scan to see what the uterus is like,' I said.

I was keen to learn more about what uteruses looked like at various stages. As we moved the head over the bitch's abdomen I suddenly saw a flickering in some tissue. 'Hang on, hang on,' I said.

As we zeroed in, moving the scan very slowly, I recognised another puppy and, more important, the flickering was its heartbeat – it was alive.

What should we do now? Obviously if we left the puppy there, whatever killed its litter mates would kill it as well, and if we did a caesarean it would probably be too early in the pregnancy for it to live. So we compromised. I gave the bitch some cortisone for 24 hours, and planned for a caesarean the next morning.

The ultrasound still showed a live puppy, so we performed the caesarean and got it out. It was definitely early – its hair was not very well developed – but at least the puppy was alive.

Mrs Fraser was marvellous. She stayed awake night and day helping the bitch feed her puppy, and after seven days it had doubled its birth weight, which is what you would expect from a normal pup. When I vaccinated it six weeks later it was in superb condition. And it was a female, exactly what she had wanted. All Mrs Fraser's expectations and dreams had been realised in this one little survivor.

As I have mentioned before I've always had mixed feelings about house calls. More often than not the animal is much sicker than the owner thinks, so all the vet ends up providing is a taxi service or an ambulance service, taking it back to the clinic where proper diagnostic services are available.

But when Mr Fisher telephoned I had to concede that a house call was essential. He wanted me to come and see his discus. A discus is a goldfish shaped like a flounder on edge and is usually worth about $400-$500. Mr Fisher's fish had water behind the eye. I consulted the book, which said that water behind the eye was treated very easily by plunging a needle into the back of the orbit and sucking the liquid out.

So I arrived at Mr Fisher's house prepared to do just that. I felt obliged to tell him that my knowledge of fish was practically zero, so I was entirely at his disposal in terms of what was going to happen to it. We read the book together and it seemed reasonably clear-cut, even if I couldn't quite see how the fluid had developed behind the eye and suspected that this might be of considerable significance.

But Mr Fisher was adamant that simply removing the fluid would be the only treatment that was necessary. So we netted the fish out of the tank – and it was quite big, about four inches long – and laid it on a wet tea towel, the only means of restraint and anaesthetic that I could devise. Without further ado I plunged the needle into the back of the discus's eye and the owner fainted clean away, hitting the floor with a terrible bang.

I hastily sucked as hard as I could and plunged the fish back into the tank before turning to Mr Fisher, who'd banged his head against the side of the stove. His head was bleeding profusely and he'd knocked a tooth out. I decided that his condition was more serious than that of the fish, so I took him straight to Outpatients at the hospital.

Mr Fisher recovered fully but the fish died. I never really believed what the book advised, but what astonished me most was that someone could faint over a fish.

People sometimes say to me, 'Vets must be cleverer than doctors because they have to know about so many different kinds of animal.' Normally I nod and say, 'Well, not really,' but occasionally different species do catch me out. A woman came in with a white Muscovy duck with a great ugly red excrescence on top of its head. She was clearly very fond of it and had brought it in because it had something wrong with its cloaca. When I looked I could see about a four-inch length of tubular flesh hanging from its cloaca, which was necrotic, scabby, bruised and bleeding because the duck had been standing on it as it walked around.

I'd seen everted rectums in cats and prolapsed uteruses in cows, so I was more or less familiar with red bits hanging out of the back of animals. I decided that this must be the duck's appendix – for some ducks have three appendixes – which had turned inside out and decided to hang out of its rectum. The simple solution, I thought, would be to ligate it and cut it off, particularly as the red bit was already in a pretty bad way and was going to be a source of infection if we didn't do something.

So we cut it off and the duck didn't seem to mind at all. But I thought I had better be thorough so I sent it off to the lab.

About a week later the phone rang and the nurse said, 'It's Jim Hutton from the lab.' When I picked up the phone up, I was surprised to hear this snorting and giggling and guffawing. I said, 'David here,' rather curtly but he didn't stop, he just kept on laughing. Finally I said, 'What's the matter?'

'Well, my dear colleague,' he said. 'You've wanged off the poor duck's wanger!'

After he'd settled down he confessed that it took him a long time to find a book that referred to this particular species of duck. Most birds reproduce by what's called a cloacal kiss, when the two orifices are placed in apposition. Only a very few species of birds actually have an intromissable organ, as it's called, or a penis. The interesting thing is that the penis hasn't got a hole through the middle. It's not so much a tube as a helter-skelter – there's a flange that spirals down the outside and the semen runs down this spiral like a helter-skelter at a circus.

'You see this patch here, just in his lungs beside his heart – that white bit? I think that's why he's coughing. It's just restricted to one lobe of the lung so it's possible to remove it.'

We were looking at the X-ray of Mrs Smith's eight-year-old West Highland white who had had a cough for the last 12 months. I smiled as I remembered the contrast these X-rays made with those I had made of Jonjon 20 years earlier. Nothing here that $20,000 worth of equipment and Penny, a specially trained vet, couldn't remedy.

'It's not simple to remove lobes of lung,' I continued. 'When the chest is opened up, the anaesthetist has to breathe for the dog because the lungs collapse. The lobe of lung has to be carefully removed because there are blood vessels involved and then the airway that supplies that lung lobe has to be closed so it's airtight. The worst that can happen is that we could remove it successfully and then find that it's a cancer that might grow back.'

'Okay,' she said, 'I'm prepared for that. I really like this little dog and I think we should try.'

Murray did the surgery, Cathy did the anaesthetic, and the operation went very well. We sent the lobe of lung out to the lab, and it was Jim again who phoned with the results.

'This is very interesting,' he said. It's a bronchogenic carcinoma. We don't see this very often in dogs and in humans it's almost invariably related to smoking – this is the typical smoker's lung cancer.'

I thanked him and hung up. Ten days after the operation Mrs Smith brought in her terrier to have the stitches removed. The wound had healed well and it looked like a complete recovery.

'Tell me, Mrs Smith, do you smoke?'

'Yes I do, as a matter of fact. In the evenings the dog sits on my lap while I watch TV and I probably get through a whole packet of smokes in one night. Come to think of it, the dog probably gets as much out of a cigarette as I do.'

'You're probably right about that, because I think your smoking has given the dog lung cancer.'

The fact that I myself had recently stopped smoking gave considerable force to the sincerity of my argument.

The good news was that four years later the dog is still alive. We do X-rays of its chest every year, and so far no bad news has shown up. Mrs Smith hasn't given up smoking, but she smokes outside now.

Mrs Shaffrey's cat was named Sid, and Sid had a huge abscess. The whole of one side of his massive tom cat head was distended with pus. 'What we should do here,' I said, 'is give Sid an anaesthetic and drain all the pus out and then put in a rubber drain to keep the hole open for a couple of days. And I think what we should do at the same time is castrate Sid. I think his testicles are really getting him into trouble. This is the third fight he's had so far his year, so I think it's important to castrate him.'

'Well,' said Mrs Shaffrey, 'I'm happy for you to drain the abscess and I've listened carefully to what you've said about the castration, but I'd really rather not.'

'But it's affecting his health.'

'Perhaps, but I insist that he's not castrated. Let me explain. When my husband was alive he once told me that if he ever died he wanted to come back as a tom cat, because they had so much fun. I didn't think anything of this at the time, but then some months later he did die quite unexpectedly. I was absolutely devastated. We had been the closest of friends and I really missed him. After the funeral was over and all the friends had gone and I was all alone, the pain was quite excruciating.'

I nodded in sympathy.

'Shortly after, I was walking up my drive one day feeling very lonely and lost, and there on the fence was this cat. It suddenly came back to me what my husband had said, and I called out to the cat without even thinking, I called out my husband's name, "Sid". Well, the cat got down off the fence, walked up to me, rubbed its head all round my legs, and then took me on a tour of the garden. The garden was my husband's real pleasure and it was lovely. We had both shared in it, but the cat took me to my husband's parts of the garden – the vegetables and the shrubs, and the roses that he pruned. He then led me inside, and it was quite eerie.

'I got a bowl of milk and put it down on the floor. The cat looked up at me and miaowed. Oh, I thought, and put the bowl on the table where my husband ate his meals. The cat hopped up onto my husband's seat, put his front feet on the table and drank the milk. He decided to stay on in the house. He sat in Sid's armchair, slept on his side of the bed and would look at me in the same way Sid had.'

'Much as I'm sympathetic and much as I wish it could be your husband, realistically I don't think it is,' I said.

'You're wrong,' she said. 'I have no doubt it's my husband. The one thing that finally persuaded me was when I got a dirt box for him. I found an old baking dish, filled it with sawdust, and put some newspaper under it. The cat got up and walked over, nodding and

purring in appreciation, climbed
into the pan, scratched round for
a while and peed over the side. I
knew then that this really was my
husband, reincarnated.'

I had known Mrs Tennant and
her daughter for a long time, the
daughter for longer than the
mother, because I treated both
her horse and her dog. Mum
would occasionally accompany
her daughter when she came in
with the dog, which she seemed
to dislike, and sometimes she

*I knew then that this really was
my husband, reincarnated.*

would be down at the paddock when I called to look at the horse,
which seemed to make her nervous.

Then one day she came in with the dog to tell me that her daughter had been killed in an accident with the horse. She looked heart-
broken and crumpled, quite unlike the tough, brittle lady that I'd
known over the years.

'You know,' she said, 'this dog and I never got on but in the last
few weeks, as I've sat on the sofa in tears, sobbing for hour after
hour, the dog has crept up on the sofa – something I never allowed
– and wheedled its way under my arm till I suddenly find I've got my
face buried in its fur and I'm weeping. Without this dog I would
have killed myself. The comfort that it gives me is unbelievable. I
don't understand how it knows what I need.'

I don't understand either, but I love the fact that it does understand what she needs.

Mr Steinberg and his dog didn't get on very well with Mrs Steinberg. It wasn't that there was anything wrong with the dog, it was more a problem with Mrs Steinberg. I never met her, but I spoke to her on the phone several times and she was always very abrupt and bitter and resentful. I suppose it was because I was always talking about the dog, who was the prime focus of her resentment. The main problem, said Mrs Steinberg, was that the dog urinated inside the house. No she didn't, said Mr Steinberg, she only occasionally wet the bed and when she did it was on a plastic sheet that he put down under the bed. Mrs Steinberg said that the house smelled; Mr Steinberg swore that it didn't.

We tried a range of treatments to control the bed wetting, which in most cases in middle-aged female dogs is because they have been spayed. The hormone from the ovaries helps maintain the strength and tone of the neck of the bladder, so without the ovaries the strength of the bladder eventually deteriorates a little. In 90 per cent of the dogs affected in this way, replacing the hormone with tablets resolves the problem – but not with Mr Steinberg's dog; it continued to wet the bed. We tried other drugs in conjunction with the female hormone, but again we were unsuccessful – the dog still wet the bed. Nowadays there's surgery during which a sling is placed under the neck of the bladder and the strength of the neck restored, but in those days if the tablets didn't work you either put up with it or put the dog down.

Unfortunately, Mr Steinberg was prevailed upon by his wife to do the latter, so he brought the dog in, saying that he couldn't bear to stay while I did the deed, the pain was too much for him. As he left he said, 'I think we're putting the wrong bitch down.'

Because some people see me as a sympathetic personality I am often asked to do house calls to euthanase dogs. I'm in favour of putting pets down at home. The dog is more comfortable; the owner doesn't have to face a waiting room of people seen dimly through tears; there's no suggestion that they have to write out a cheque on the spot, and they can sit with the body of their dear friend as long as they like before they arrange a funeral.

Mr and Mrs Shaw owned a beautiful, vivacious, elegant, long-haired german shepherd. Some german shepherds, as they get older, develop a condition in which the nerve supply to the hind legs and finally the hind end of the body, deteriorates. The disease is called german shepherd myelopathy. The early signs are a slight lack of coordination in the back legs. Later, the dog will stand on top of its back feet without being aware of it and will tangle its back legs up going round corners. It is relentlessly progressive, takes about two years, and always ends in euthanasia.

The great sadness is that the mental ability and the front end of the dog are completely unaffected. The dogs remain cheerful and they are in no pain, but eventually they start to drop faeces and they develop a paralysed bladder, so that they leak urine all the time and get bladder infections. Ultimately they develop bed-sores, even in the best nursed dogs, because urine scalds the skin on which the dog is lying and it erodes and finally ulcerates. It is desirable to put the dog down before this time but this decision is always devastating for an owner, having to look at that alert, smiling face and the shambling, dragging, soiled back end.

Mr and Mrs Shaw's dog developed this condition. We had discussed the prospects of euthanasia and when to do it several times. Finally they decided.

Mr. Shaw was unable to stay home to face the death of his beloved pet. He dug a hole and left. Mrs Shaw and I gave her dog its fatal injection. She was very brave. I picked the dog up and she led the way down the path to where the hole had been dug. It was about six foot long by about four foot wide and about four feet deep. The bottom had been carefully covered in straw. I was faced with a dilemma, standing there holding the dog in my arms. My back was starting to hurt, but it seemed wrong to just drop the dog so far down into the bottom of the hole. So the only thing I could do was to jump in with him. At that point I realised that the straw had been placed there because the water table was only about three feet from the surface. I sank into the mud up to my knees. Eventually I managed to scramble out, and together we buried the dog.

Lyttelton Engineering made barbecues manufactured from 40-gallon drums cut lengthways, with grates welded over the opening. What had begun as sideline soon became the firm's stock-in-trade. The drums had originally been used for storing fat for supply to fish and chip shops and this was the fatal attraction for the young cat that had trapped itself inside the half-finished barbecue. When I arrived its head was caught in the bung hole on the end of the drum. It was a little feral cat and alternated between spitting and asphyxiating itself as it pulled furiously back in an attempt to escape.

'What we want you to do, Doc,' said the yard foreman, 'is give it a jab and keep it asleep while we hacksaw a piece out of the bung hole.'

I was impressed that they were quite prepared to sacrifice their barbecue for the sake of this little wild kitten – I had expected them to ask me to put the cat down. After a struggle I found a vein and was able to inject a new drug called Saffan, which worked very well. I taped the half-filled syringe to the cat's leg so that I could add more drug as needed and anxiously watched her chest rise and fall over the three-quarters of an hour it took to hacksaw the bung apart.

The workers stood back to let me lift the kitten out once the job was done and crowded around proudly to see the result. I was suddenly aghast to discover that the cat had stopped breathing, but knew it hadn't been long because I'd been watching her very carefully.

'Look out,' I said. I knelt down and put my mouth over the front part of her head and began to breathe into her. The cat vomited. Memories of Bridget flooded back. In tears I continued to breathe and push on her stomach. 'Please let me win this time,' I murmured to my hated enemy, God. It took a long time but the kitten did finally recover. They wrote about it in the local paper, mentioning the tears as a sign of my passionate determination to save the cat, describing me as a hero. They had no idea how painful that moment was for me.

The vicar of St John's had a golden labrador he called Eli and the publican at the Occidental had a rottweiler he called Satan. Both dogs were exercised in Latimer Square, so it was inevitable that one day there would be a confrontation. Predictably, the golden retriever lost the battle, and the vicar brought him in so I could repair the bite wounds and a torn ear. We anaesthetised Eli, put drains in the bite wounds and sutured up the ear.

Some time later the publican from the Occidental came in with his rottweiler, which had developed terribly swollen testicles. When we looked closely we discovered that buried in the swollen tissue was a rubber band. The swelling and the damage were so severe that the dog had to be castrated, which wasn't a bad idea anyway, because Satan was starting to reach middle age and his prostate would probably play up.

I told the vicar all about it when he came in to have Eli vaccinated. He blushed slightly when I told him how Satan had had to be castrated.

'God works in mysterious ways,' he said, 'his miracles to perform.'

Father O'Connor from Lyttelton, on the other hand, was much more concerned about my survival in the after-life. In the early 1970s a drug called Arecolin was used for treating hydatids. It caused a violent reaction in the dog's gut, at the same time inducing a temporary paralysis of the worm, so the worm was ejected in the middle of a great heap of mucus. Some dogs suffered severe gut pain and spasms and became quite distressed. Father O'Connor's elderly malamute fell into this category, and when the time came for his treatment the priest became almost as distressed as the dog.

It was possible for a vet to write a certificate exempting dogs from this form of dosing if they had a suitable disease, but the old malamute was remarkably healthy and it was very difficult, in all conscience, to write such a certificate. Each time the dog was dosed it had a more severe reaction and each time the good Father would become more beseeching. I finally relented and gave my certificate in return for Father O'Connor's certificate guaranteeing me absolution on my death and an assured entrance into Heaven. I am not sure who had to tell the greater lie.

I have specified in my will that this document is to be taped to the lid of my coffin, in full view of God as we enter the church, so that the hateful old bastard has no option but to let me in.

12

Of Leopards and Lions

Bill Gray was the owner of a small zoo at North Beach on the eastern side of Christchurch. The zoo was always a favourite weekend visiting place for many of Christchurch's children, and more by default than anything else I became its veterinarian.

The first time I met Bill was when I was still working for Roy, who sent me down to trim the hooves of some Fallabella ponies that Bill had as part of his zoo. One of the ponies had kicked Bill in the crutch and Bill, who was a very tough and capable person, gave up any thought of doing the hooves at that stage.

Bill had started off with a collection of otters and fish and two small crocodiles. They had been there since I was a child. One of these died when quite young, but the one remaining croc occupied an important place in his exhibits. Later a visiting circus went broke so he acquired a tiger, two leopards and a lion.

I had absolutely no training or knowledge of large cats so I was quite taken aback when Bill rang to say that one of the leopards was sick and could I come and treat it? After we had observed this sick-looking, lethargic leopard for some time Bill decided that it had probably eaten a piece of sack he'd thrown into the animal's pen.

'Well, there's only one way to check,' I said, 'and that's to dart it.'

John Thompson, a local veterinary wholesaler who for some reason had a dart gun, was happy to have a go, although he had never actually darted a leopard before. The leopard was sitting in the middle of the enclosure when he arrived, so John put his rifle through the netting and pulled the trigger, striking the leopard's leg. All very good. After roaring a bit and running around the cage for about ten minutes it lay down and went to sleep.

At the back of the enclosure was a double door. Bill ushered me through the first door, shut it firmly behind me and said, 'Away you go.'

So in I went in, not feeling as confident as I looked. Nor was I totally convinced the big cat was asleep. I reached out and touched it on the eye with a long stick. Nothing happened. I then kicked its

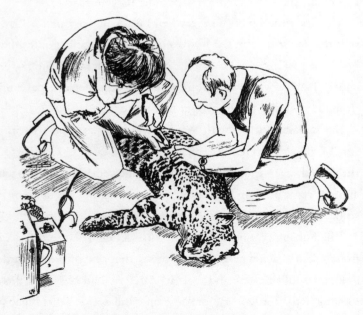

I was not totally convinced that the big cat was really asleep.

back legs, on the basis that these were the parts furthest from its mouth. I then plucked up sufficient courage to take a blood sample from a vein in its back leg and hurriedly inject some antibiotics and vitamin B before it had a chance to wake up. I delicately felt its abdomen – nothing wrong there. I listened to its chest – everything seemed to be okay. I moved towards its head, felt all around the glands of its neck, pulled back its lips and looked at its teeth.

Again everything seemed normal so I thought, well, I'm going to have to have a look down its throat. I took hold of the leopard's head, opened its jaws, pulled its tongue out and looked down its throat. At that very moment it let out a guttural, absolutely sincere growl from deep down in its gut. I dropped the head, grabbed all my gear and flew out of the cage.

Eventually the leopard made an uneventful recovery. The blood test was normal, and Bill decided that it had simply become love-sick for the lion, which was on heat in the next-door cage.

Over a period of time all of Bill's big animals got sick. The two leopards had a fight, with the result that the loser became badly infected, depressed, dehydrated and moribund. This was perhaps my most hair-raising visit to the zoo, for the animal was too sick to anaesthetise. Bill held its head down with a broom while I put a drip in its leg. It growled and hissed and carried on under the broom, but fortunately was too weak to move. With the aid of the broom we got a bag of fluids into it along with some antibiotics, but it died soon afterwards. All the time I was injecting the drip I kept remembering all the books I had read saying that leopards were the most unreliable and unpredictable of the big cats.

Susan the lion was Bill's favourite. He would join Susan in her cage and play with her, sometimes showing off by putting his head in her mouth. He invited me to join him on several occasions, but I steadfastly refused. So it was a real concern when Susan became sick, really seriously sick. She simply lay around the cage, refusing to eat or drink.

I talked to Lindsay Fraser, the vet for Orana Park – the other place in town with lots of lions – who told me of the time he'd darted out a lion and done a blood test. He decided that its kidneys had failed and put it down, only to discover at the post mortem that the problem was a foreign body – a great big piece of bark.

To dart out Susan, Bill had borrowed a dart gun from a friend. He assumed that I knew how to use it, which I didn't, but luckily there was a book of instructions in the bag. My main problem was to work out how hard the dart should hit the lion to penetrate the skin. These dart guns are based on a .22 blank, the gas of which forces the dart out the front. There was a valve on the side of the barrel that allowed some of the gas to leak, thus controlling the velocity of the dart.

Bill gave me an old sports coat – an old suit coat, I think it was – that we hung on the hedge and we spent about an hour adjusting the dial on the valve to get the dart to just penetrate the coat without going any further. After our experiments it was clear the coat was never going to be worn again – some of the darts went right through both the coat and the hedge.

The greatest difficulty with zoo animals is to work out the correct dose of anaesthetic. Here was Susan, an overweight and sick lioness – how on earth was I to decide the correct dosage? First we had to guess the weight of the lion, and it was a total guess – she could have been anywhere between 200 and 400kg. Then we had to reduce the dose because she was ill. Finally I had to come up with a dose that would fit inside a single syringe.

Using the dart gun was going to be a total act of faith. I stuck the gun through the netting and pulled the trigger. The look of horror and distrust on the lion's face was more than a little upsetting. Here was one of the humans who had always looked after her and loved her aiming a gun at her and actually hurting her. She walked round the cage for ten minutes or so, occasionally casting me a hurt and sorrowful look, then lay down.

Bill went in with me because he reckoned he could trust this lion. Again I poked her gently with a stick, but she didn't move. Indeed she was barely breathing and looked dangerously ill. At that stage the nurses and helpers who had been looking on all crowded into the cage. This was not a good moment for a vet. What if the animal suddenly decided to wake up? How many people would get mauled before we could do anything?

But Susan seemed to be so thoroughly asleep I thought she might be in danger of dying. We set up a drip in a vein, with one of the helpers holding the bag. The idea was that we would put additional anaesthetic in the drip if she appeared to be waking up.

We then took our blood samples. The blood urea was up a bit, but that was probably because she was dehydrated. I then felt around her tummy and thought I could feel an enlargement, a solid mass that could have been a tumour, so without delay I decided to do an exploratory operation and have a look inside her abdomen.

We turned her on her back, clipped her hair and sterilised the skin. Altogether the nurse and I were well organised for this – we had all the skin sterilising material as well as autoclave packs of instruments, so the standard of hygiene was almost as good as in an operating theatre. We draped the abdomen with sterile drapes and all too soon we were ready to make the first incision. It was then that I discovered that lion's skin is much tougher than you'd think. Even with brand-new scalpel blades I was struggling to get through.

Finally I penetrated the abdomen. Looking back I suppose that this was no more difficult a piece of surgery than operating on a very large dog, but it was a very large abdomen. The first thing I noticed were traces of pus around the organs. Oh goodness, I thought, there's something wrong here.

Pus suggests more infection than tumour, so we kept poking around until I came across the uterus, which was both distended and engorged. The ovaries also had traces of pus around them. I then diagnosed that the uterus had become infected with pyometra, which as I have described earlier simply means a uterus full of pus – a common condition in cats and dogs. In this case small amounts of pus were leaking out of the fallopian tube – the connection between the uterus and the ovaries.

It wasn't a difficult task to tie off Susan's ovaries and blood vessels and remove the whole ovary and uterus, as we would with a dog or a cat with this condition. We closed her up and gave her antibiotics, put on another bag of drip and sat to wait. By late evening she hadn't moved and it was starting to get cold, so we dragged Suzy into her enclosure, put sacks and blankets under and over her and installed an electric heater.

The next morning Susan woke up and smashed the heater with one swipe of her paw. She was clearly feeling much better. It took a further five days for her to start to eat, but she continued to drink, and once she got food inside her the improvement was dramatic. Bill was delighted with the result. I think if Susan had died he would have given up the zoo altogether.

Albert the monkey was an entirely different proposition. Bill's wife Trish had become expert at raising orphan moneys – they were the most delightful, cuddly characters you could imagine, but tended to be a bit destructive and messy when they ran around the house, jumping from curtain rail to curtain rail.

But as adults the monkeys had no great respect for their keepers, tending to regard them as equals, and Bill had a lot of difficulty with this particular one, which had bitten him several times when he tried to clean out the runs. Albert was also far too aggressive with his troupe of female monkeys, several of whom had been severely injured. Once we had remove two fingers and sew up the hand of one female who had put her hand under the wire, allowing Albert to bite the fingers off. .

So Bill decided that the only way to deal with Albert was to remove the big eye teeth that did most of the damage. A dart gun was not really feasible, because there weren't any muscle masses large enough for the dart to penetrate without causing injury, so we developed a new plan.

Bill's son was enlisted to use a banana to entice the monkey to put its arm through the wires of the cage. The plan was that he would then grab the arm and hold on tight with his foot up against the wire, pulling the arm right out through to the armpit. I was then to give the monkey an anaesthetic and after that had taken effect Bill was to enter the cage and pick up the monkey, now fast asleep, while Trish stood by with the hose.

The first part of the plan worked okay – well, not quite okay. The son pulled so hard that he injured the monkey's arm, which was never quite the same again. I managed to inject the anaesthetic and Bill was there to catch the anaesthetised monkey. But to our astonishment the females, far from being relieved at having this wife-basher of a monkey taken from their midst, rose up at this gross intrusion on their family unit, suddenly launching themselves on Bill en masse.

Trish bravely set to with the hose, but she was so upset and excited that the only person she managed to squirt was Bill – none of the female monkeys seemed to have any water on them at all. Bill was left struggling alone with an anaesthetised monkey in one arm while fighting off a troop of enraged female monkeys with the other.

We finally got Albert inside the house, where after a long battle extracting his firmly embedded teeth out of his jaw we sat back to wait for him to recover. This took much longer than I had expected, and finally I had to return to the clinic and get a drip to ensure that he didn't dehydrate. I decided that it would also help to flush the anaesthetic out of his system faster.

Albert stayed inside in a cage with Bill sitting up with him the whole night. The monkey recovered, but his arm was never quite the same again. It worked, but it wasn't as strong as the other one.

The worst day during my relationship with Bill came with the illness of the tiger he had also managed to acquire from the small circus that went broke. According to Bill, this tiger was notorious. There had been newspaper reports of prints on the sand at Karaki Beach that looked very similar to those of a tiger, and the local vet had collected faeces that were supposedly tiger faeces, and had found worms that would occur only in tiger faeces. Bill said the previous owner had admitted that this particular tiger had indeed walked on Karaki Beach.

As always seemed to happen with these large zoo animals, the tiger just stopped eating one day. We tried antibiotics in the food, but the tiger still wouldn't eat, so things just spiralled downwards. It soon became obvious that we would have to dart the tiger, so we went through the same business with the dart gun and the coat until we felt we had the right strength of gas in the gun. But when I aimed at the tiger and pulled the trigger I immediately realised that something had gone wrong. The valve must have been bumped, because the gun made a much louder noise than I expected, and the dart was nowhere to be seen.

The tiger lay down and went to sleep, and it was only when I took a closer look at her that I realised the dart had gone through the muscly part of her thigh and embedded itself in her abdomen. This was not a good start, and things didn't get better when we felt a lump in her abdomen which after surgery turned out to be a terminal tumour. So we put the poor tiger down.

We both felt bad about the tiger's death and went inside Bill's house to have a few drinks. I felt sorry for Bill, so I suggested he come back home with me and have a cup of tea. He had separated from his wife by this time, and I didn't really think he should be left alone on his own.

When we arrived back at our house Bill was a little the worse for wear. He climbed the steps through the garden to our front door, where he stood admiring the view over the estuary. He had just started to say how marvellous it was when he toppled forwards into the garden and crashed through the shrubbery, becoming stuck in several large bushes near the bottom of the slope. I went down and dragged him out from the bottom of the garden. We started up the path again with my hand on his shoulder, but I lost my grip and, incredibly, down he went down into the bushes once more.

By this time Faye had realised that her husband was home, accompanied apparently by some undesirable friends, so she was looking distinctly frosty when we started up the path for the third time. But she came and helped when she realised it was old Bill, and we brought him inside and tidied him up. He was cut and scratched and really in quite a sorry state, so we patched him up, gave him a cup of tea and put him to bed.

For the last ten years of the mini-zoo's life Bill was regularly harassed by a group of people called SAFE, who considered the zoo to be cruel to animals. I was always of the opinion that as most of the animals had come from circuses and other zoos they would never have survived in a large open zoo like Orana Park. They were kept in scrupulously clean quarters and were fed as much as they could eat. Their veterinary treatment was as prompt and comprehensive as we could make it.

There was never any suggestion that Bill would do anything but his very best for these animals, but finally he had to close his zoo and sell up. Happily none of the animals had to be put down; they were all re-housed in zoos in various parts of New Zealand. Susan, by virtue of a subscription from the people of Christchurch, had a special enclosure built for her at Orana Park, where sadly she also recently died.

The mini-zoo is no more a place of enjoyment for a large number of Christchurch's children, and a particularly important and nostalgic part of my life has also disappeared.

13

Ducks, Fish ...
and Franz Kafka

Recently I took up duck shooting, partly in response to all the gundog owners who brought their dogs in and my belief that one of the best ways to understand people's problems is to take part in the activity that produces them. So I first acquired a gun and then a dog. I was quite keen on the idea of going quail shooting as well as ducks, so I decided to get a pointer rather than a labrador.

The difference between a labrador and a pointer is monumental. Labradors retrieve; pointers do almost everything else – at about 100mph. But I finally got this dog trained to the point where it would occasionally bring back a duck, so off the three of us set on our first hunting expedition to the West Coast – my son Matthew, my dog Willy and I.

After a surprisingly successful morning we went off with the local duckshooters to the pub. I was happily sipping my beer in a corner when I was approached by a woman I immediately recognised, as she had been bringing her rooster, Tegel, into the clinic for some time. Tegel was a lucky bird; he had either fallen off or had been dragged from a crate on the back of a truck on its way to the poultry processing plant.

This woman was a great enthusiast on the subject of animal welfare and, like many enthusiastic people, she spoke very quickly and volubly.

'Oh,' she said, 'how nice to meet you here. We've just had a most exciting morning. We've been at Lake Mahinapua scaring the ducks off so that the duckshooters won't get them. We've had placards and smoke-bombs and we've been out in boats – it's been terrific fun.'

'Great,' I said weakly, wishing either she or I were somewhere else. I waited for her to say it. 'And what have you been doing here?'

I had my answer prepared. 'Oh, we've just been tramping and observing nature and taking photographs and generally enjoying the wonders that nature can provide.'

With impeccable timing Matthew burst through the door at that moment. 'Dad, Dad, come outside!' he shouted. 'Willy's just eaten all our ducks!'

Trout fishing is a sport that one can easily become passionate about. It has many advantages and virtually no disadvantages. It's a form of escapism. It gets you to country you would never go to otherwise. You don't even have to be successful at it, although it's desirable. It's not competitive, and best of all it attracts a very interesting and thoughtful group of exponents.

I started fishing when I was about ten, having saved up enough money by doing jobs for the neighbours to buy my first reel – a Mitchell Cap, I remember, a lovely piece of engineering – and a rod. The sports shop got to know me quite well because I would sit there for hours, studying the flies and reading the catalogues. Happily they were quite an encouraging group of men behind the counter.

The Avon River was my regular fishing spot. I could bike there after school and stay fishing till probably 9 o'clock at night. In those

days it wasn't unsafe for a ten-year-
old boy to be on the banks of the
river in Hagley Park at night. The
Avon River fish were, however,
very educated. My favourite fly was
a Red Shadow – a mainly black fly
with a small piece of red on it. It
would invariably attract fish out
from under the weeds, which
would follow the fly until they
got close to the bank, when
they would spot me and veer
off and disappear.

This happened so often
that it gave me an idea. I tied
a piece of metre-long nylon

You don't even have to be successful at fishing, but it is desirable.

on to the back of my Red Shadow, to which I attached a bare treble
hook. I'd noticed that if I let the fly drop during the retrieve the fish
would swing across the line of the fly's retrieval before vanishing
underneath the bank. So my theory was that as the fish swung across
the line I could draw the treble hook sharply into the fish's abdomen, or whatever part of the fish was nearby.

It worked a treat. In the end I had to be fairly selective because I
found myself catching so many fish.

I remember fishing from the Antigua boatshed bridge one day –
there were always lots of fish under there. An old chap was watching
over my shoulder and said, 'Look! One's interested in your fly.' He
could see this trout following the fly up from the bottom. Then,
with puzzlement in his voice as I allowed the fly to sink below the
fish, he said, 'You'll never catch a fish like ... my God, you've got

him!' He hadn't noticed the dexterity with which I foul-hooked the trout, which after a terrible struggle I landed about six yards downstream, out of view of my elderly observer.

I took up fishing again seriously as an adult after Bridget died, mainly because it was restful and not competitive. Once again I became very enthusiastic, even deciding to tie my own flies and attending a fly-tying class run by John Morton, who was a very good teacher.

I went fishing with my first creations to the Maruia on the West Coast. This is a lovely river that glides along through farmland. It's always clear and holds lovely big trout. I spotted a beautiful trout in a ripple. Every now and then I could see its mouth break the surface of the water as it took dry flies, so here was a perfect opportunity to try out my new creation. As I cast forward with the final pass and the fly sped past my shoulder its two wings fluttered gently down to the water in front of me. The remains of the fly landed very accurately about a metre in front of the trout, exactly where I intended it to go. As it meandered back towards me, miraculously still floating in the eddies of the current, the fish fidgeted slightly and then majestically began to rise. Its mouth opened centimetres beneath the fly and it started to move forward to take it just when the hackle began to unwind. I could see the fish's eyes widen in amazement, great white orbs, and then it shot first to the bottom of the river and then upstream as fast as it could. You could actually see its bow wave as it sped off.

The south branch of the Waimakariri, which runs behind the Belfast Hotel, is another very attractive river. I was fishing there one evening on the bank behind a large hay barn just as it was starting to become dark. Out in front of me in the darkness was a periodic loud splash – this was a very big fish. I tried repeatedly to land my fly in the right place but most of my casts got tangled in the dark.

Finally the fly got caught in the undergrowth so I had to break the trace. But I was determined to keep trying to catch this fish because it sounded enormous. I'd forgotten to bring a torch but I had some matches, so I lit a small fire out of dry hay from the shed, which gave me sufficient light to tie on more tippet material, not without difficulty, and attach a big white fly that was meant to represent a moth.

This took about an hour in the flickering light, but finally everything was ready and I ran my fingers back up the line, both to check that everything was secure and to find my rod, which was out there somewhere in the dark. I got part-way along the fly line when it disappeared from between my fingers. Somehow I had managed to burn through the line with my little signal fire. I gave up in disgust and went home.

I was fishing on the Coast when the farmer came down the track with a message. 'Faye's rung,' he said. 'Dick Dean's been killed.'

The quiet pleasure and solitude of the fishing stream dissolved.

The next day I flew to Auckland, stopping on the way at Wellington, where two of my friends who were also friends of Dick, joined me on the flight. Once in Auckland we hired a rental car and drove to Whangaparaoa.

It was a very sad funeral. I cried when they sang 'E'en though I walk in death's dark vale I will fear no ill.' I cried for Dick, but I cried more for myself, for this was the hymn that was sung at Bridget's funeral, and that was a phrase that would go through my head as I stood on the back lawn at Maffeys Road, staring up at the sky.

After the funeral Dick's widow Janet invited some of us to stay for a walk around the farm and a drink. My friends had to be on the plane to Wellington by 10pm and my direct flight to Christchurch was 20 minutes later. I barely recall arriving at Auckland airport. I had obviously drunk too much, but I think I was stunned and exhausted as well.

When I awoke at 3 o'clock in the morning I realised that I wasn't at home. I had no idea where I was, but it certainly wasn't my bedroom. I was not much clearer when a man came into the room and offered me a plate of toast, saying, 'We can't leave you here on your own. It's time we went and did our rounds.' So I threw the blanket back and got up. Beyond the room I was sleeping in was an office, and it was only then that I realised I was in a police station.

'You fell asleep at the airport,' the officer said. 'We've phoned your wife.'

'Oh,' I said, 'how did you get the number?'

'You had credit cards in your pocket – we weren't sure if they were yours or not, so we tracked down your address and phone number on our computer. When we phoned your wife we said we had this dishevelled-looking fellow who was asleep and drunk at Auckland airport – did she think it was her husband? We were a bit surprised when she replied immediately, without hesitation, "Oh yes, that'll be him".'

I was surprised as well, because this was the one and only time I'd ever failed to catch an aeroplane or keep an appointment.

We set off in the police car through the streets of Mangere back towards Auckland airport, and as we were leaving one of the policemen turned and said, 'Did you have any luggage?'

'No,' I said, 'just the clothes I have on.'

'Well, you must have been pretty cold.'

I looked down and discovered I had no jacket and was dressed only in a shirt and tie. 'Oh,' I said, 'I had a sports coat – in fact it's quite a new sports coat.'

'Okay,' he said. So we drove round to the rental car place and along the row of cars until I recognised the one that we had hired. 'Luckily,' he said, 'they don't clean them out till the morning. Hang on.' He shone his torch in and there in the back seat was my jacket. The window had been left partly down so there was no difficulty in opening the back door and retrieving it. Inside the coat was my plane ticket.

'Come on,' he said, 'we'll take you for a Tiki tour of Mangere.' Ten minutes down the road he pointed off to his right and said, 'That's where our Prime Minister lives, David Lange.'

We'd been touring for about three-quarters of an hour when they had a message on their radio: 'We want you to go and attend a disturbance in a house. Apparently there's a chap there with an aggressive dog.'

'Fine,' said one of the policemen, 'we've got a vet in the back. This'll be no trouble to us.'

We pulled up at a tenement house – a two-storeyed weatherboard state house with a door at the front and a little porch. 'The dog's upstairs,' said the woman who answered the door. So the two policemen and I marched up the stairs. In the bedroom on a bed lay a large Samoan man holding down a heap of blankets that pulsed and throbbed occasionally.

'Where's the dog?' they asked.

'Under here,' said the man.

Both policemen looked at me for advice. 'What should we do?'

'Take out your gun and just shoot it straight through the blankets,' I said.

This was not the answer they were expecting. One of the officers escorted me back to the car and sat me down on the back seat. Some time later the other policeman came out of the house. He had managed to settle the man and his dog down without having to do any damage to the dog.

Dawn was breaking as we drove back to the police station at the airport. 'Have a shower. We'll lend you a razor. Get yourself tidied up. We've got you booked on a plane at 8 o'clock.' They drove me to the terminal and pulled up outside the departure hall.

'We know your friend has died, and we know what pain you're feeling, but please try and behave better in future,' one of the officers said.

'Yes,' I said, 'yes,' starting to feel the first pangs of alcoholic remorse.

As I turned to go he added, 'You haven't heard of a chap called Franz Kafka by any chance, have you?'

14

Flicking the Switch

My mother often said that she thought that I would be either an absent-minded professor or a total failure. I'm just so pleased that she had the perception to choose a middle path when she decided so many years ago that I should be a vet. Being a vet has allowed me to be whimsical, forgetful, vague and enthusiastic – qualities I have in abundance but which, in almost any other career, would have produced Mum's alternative prediction.

Educationists may question the value of bomb-making skills as a preparation for life, but in Mum's mind this fell into the same category as viewing paramecium under a microscope. Anything that fostered our curiosity, with the exception of other people's genitals, was to be strongly encouraged and, as all her three sons graduated from university, it is hard to deny the value of her methods. Mum was just as successful in her choice of careers for her other two sons. Fortunately they had more ability in the real world and John became an objective and skilful scientist and Ken a successful lawyer.

I have been delighted with Mum's choice of a career for me so far. It's been varied, interesting, even dazzling sometimes – not to mention catastrophic at others. I still enjoy getting up each morning, showering and going to work. The cup of tea when I first arrive, the abuse and heckling from all the nurses who have been such close and constant friends over a long period – these form the very substance of my life.

I am lost in admiration for my veterinary colleagues with whom I work. But the dizzying intellectual heights to which they have climbed are not always appreciated in our neighbourhood, and sometimes superb skills as a vet – the hard-won pearls of knowledge we started to garner at vet school and which we've built on ever since – are not enough.

One afternoon I came back to the clinic to find an air of anxiety and nervousness. As I walked in, Lyn said, 'The bikies are out the back with their dog.'

When I walked through to the treatment room, Pru took me to one side and said, 'They're out in the animal house. I tried to tell them what's wrong with it, but they don't seem to understand.'

'So what's happened?' I asked.

'The dog was hit by a car. I've taken an X-ray. It has a fractured L3 with cord compression. I've done all its reflexes. There's absolutely no deep pain whatsoever. There is an exaggerated patella reflex, and in the last half hour it's developed Shiff-Sherrington reflex in its front legs, which can only mean that there's an ascending haemorrhage in the cord. It won't be long before this dog is unable to breathe because its respiratory muscles are paralysed. I've told them this, but they don't seem to understand.'

'Hang on,' I said, 'I'll go and have a talk to them.'

I went into the animal house where the three bikies were sitting on the floor, each with a bottle of beer, each with their gang patches on. Between them was their dog lying on a blanket.

'Hey, Doc. What's wrong with our dog?'

'Hey, Doc,' said the one with the full moko. 'What's wrong with our dog?'

'Your dog's fucked,' I replied.

'Oh,' he said. 'Why didn't she tell us that in the first place?'

With the advent of specialists, general veterinary practices are changing now, and I am pleased to see the development, because knowledge in every area is now so great that it's probably more than one person could learn and retain to a very high standard. But I'm grateful I started practice in an era when we were called upon to do – and did – whatever was necessary in the circumstances. During the past 20 years anything that I have wanted or needed to do with small animals I have been able to do – in total contrast to human medicine. If I needed to do an operation I'd never done before, I did it. If I became interested in heart disease: I could do it. If I developed an interest in eye surgery or orthopaedics or reproduction: I could do them all.

With the quantum advance in diagnostic and treatment skills has come an improvement in the confidence with which outcomes can be predicted. As a consequence the 'art' of the vet is slipping away. The charm of an unexpected victory, or the exquisite terror of an imminent calamity is less of a possibility. This, then, is the transition from the exploding budgie in Hokitika to the lung surgery in Linwood; from the failure of the cancer eye in Fox Glacier to the success of the ultrasound at Aldwins Road.

I am content to be swept along on this tide. It is great not to have to say, 'I don't know', and our pets and livestock are definitely the better for it, even if the elimination of the mystery results in less daily drama than in the past.

Recently I took part in a bronze-casting course and was enraptured by what I saw. Here were all the themes of my life, the elements that have begun to slip away as the uncertainties have dissolved. There is fire, the risk of explosion, the uncertainty of the results, the erratic nature of the material, the possibility of brilliant success or, just as likely, cataclysmic failure. I found the pouring of the molten metal itself, with the intense, golden glow of the liquid bronze lighting our faces, an ecstatic experience.

I have begun excavations to install my own bronze foundry. Any day now I shall, once again, have the opportunity to lean forward and flick the switch.